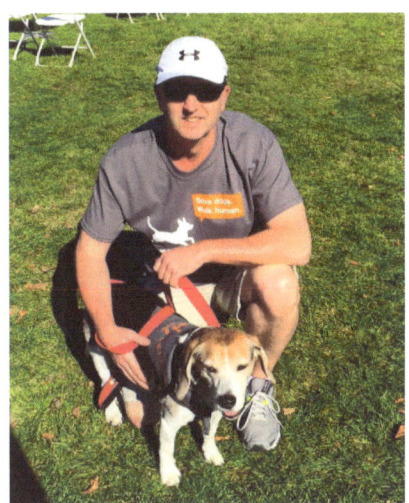

For every horror story of a dog being mistreated, abused or neglected, there is a story of redemption. A story of a dog finding it's forever home, and a life of treats, walks, chasing balls and napping.

Their story usually begins at a local shelter, pound or foster home, where alone and frightened, they are plucked from this nightmare existence by a new owner, who even after sometimes one visit, just 'knows' they will be a right fit.

Lucky enough to travel extensively, I've met many dogs. Friends with dogs, friends-of-friends with dogs, all with a story of salvation. This book is a celebration of these new beginnings – a testament to the worthy pets finding their rightful place in the world, and their kind and generous owners who find it in their heart to just take a chance.

James Wadley

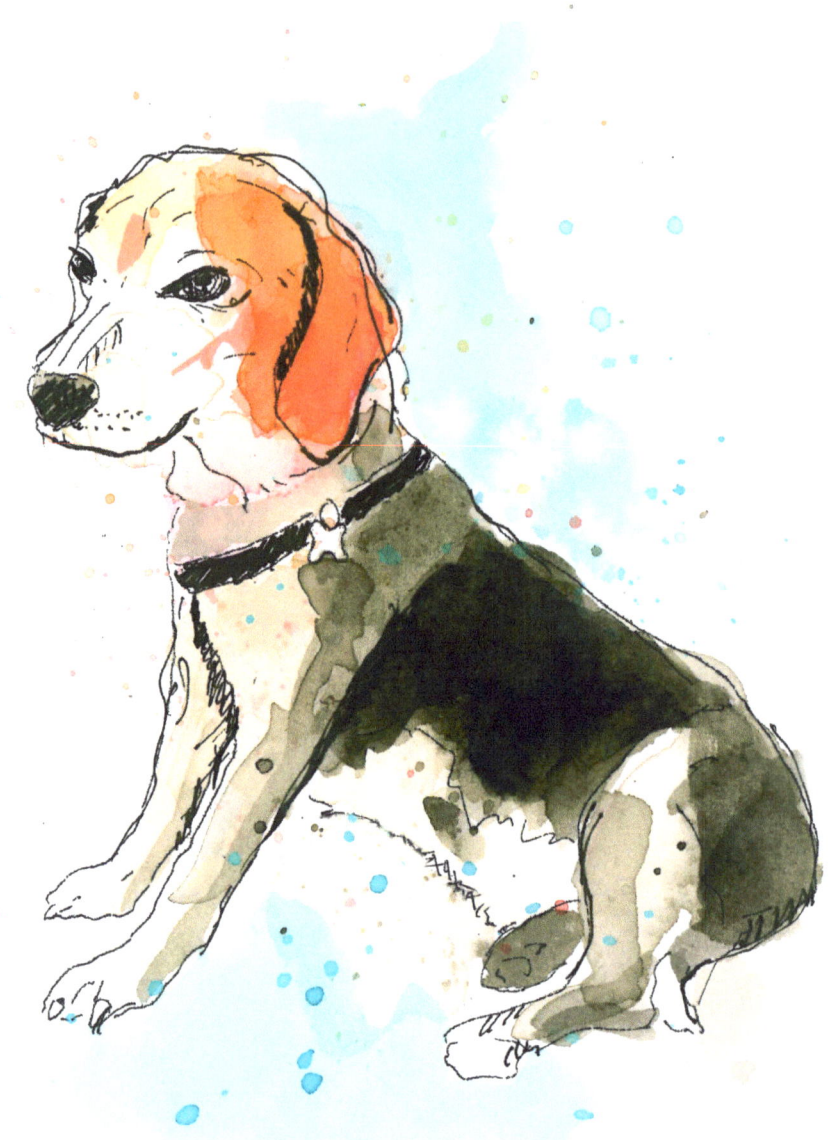

Droopy

Salt Lake City, Utah, USA

Meet Droopy – the inspiration for this book! Surrended at age three Droopy caught the eye of his new loving Mom, Melissa. The bond was instantaneous, and thus began 14 years of fun, companionship, and countless miles of hiking together through Utah's beautiful mountains and deserts. Droopy has said goodbye now, but not before proving the benefits of adopting can last a lifetime.

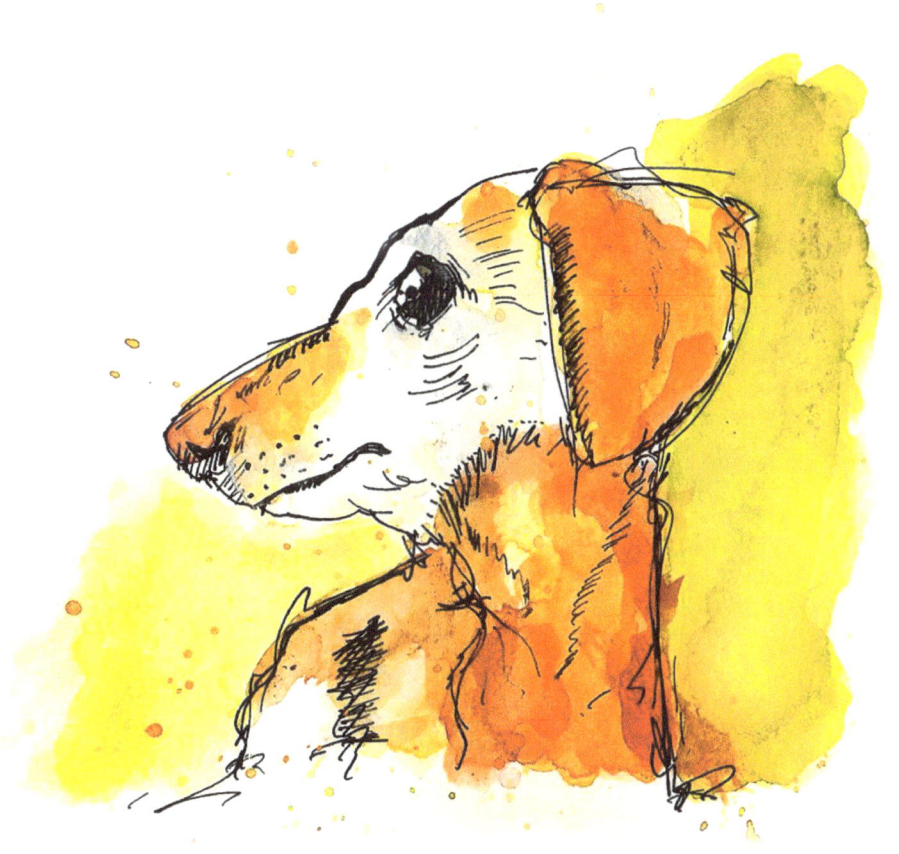

Maxwell

Anaheim, California, USA

Dachshunds are best, right? My absolute favourite. I have never met young Maxwell in the flesh, but it is a life goal. Playful and cheeky, Maxy is living the dogs life in the loving home of the Anderson family. Can you believe they found him in a pound? Who in their right mind would surrender a cutie like this? Their loss is the Anderson's gain.

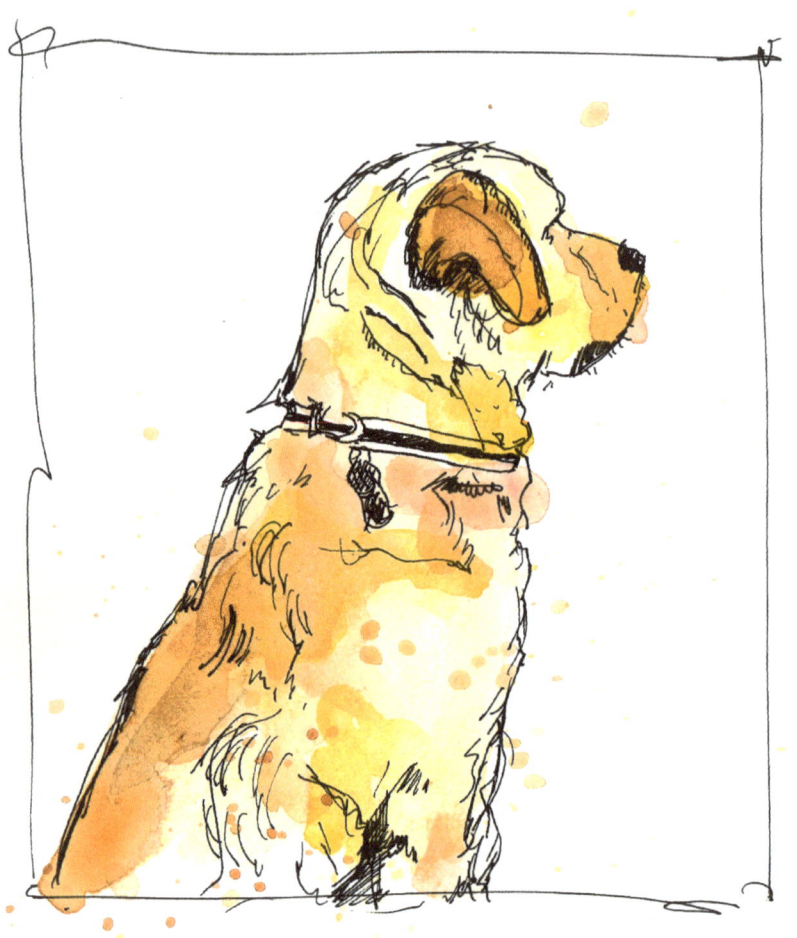

Oscar

Brisbane, Australia

It's especially sad when dogs are rescued from abuse situations. Reported by neighbours, young Oscar was removed from his unhappy home, and by way of a kind foster family, ended up in the loving arms of Donna and Phil. And he hasn't looked back. Like in other areas of modern life – if you see something, say something!

Maddison

Melbourne, Australia

This was how young Maddy was found - alone, scared and dripping wet in a suburban Melbourne park. A beautiful beagle-mix, obviously well fed and lovingly cared for, her owners failed her at the final hurdle - failing to get her microchipped! Despite an extensive social media campaign, her owners were never found, and are probably to this day wondering what became of their beautiful Maddy. Heed the warning everybody - get your pup chipped!

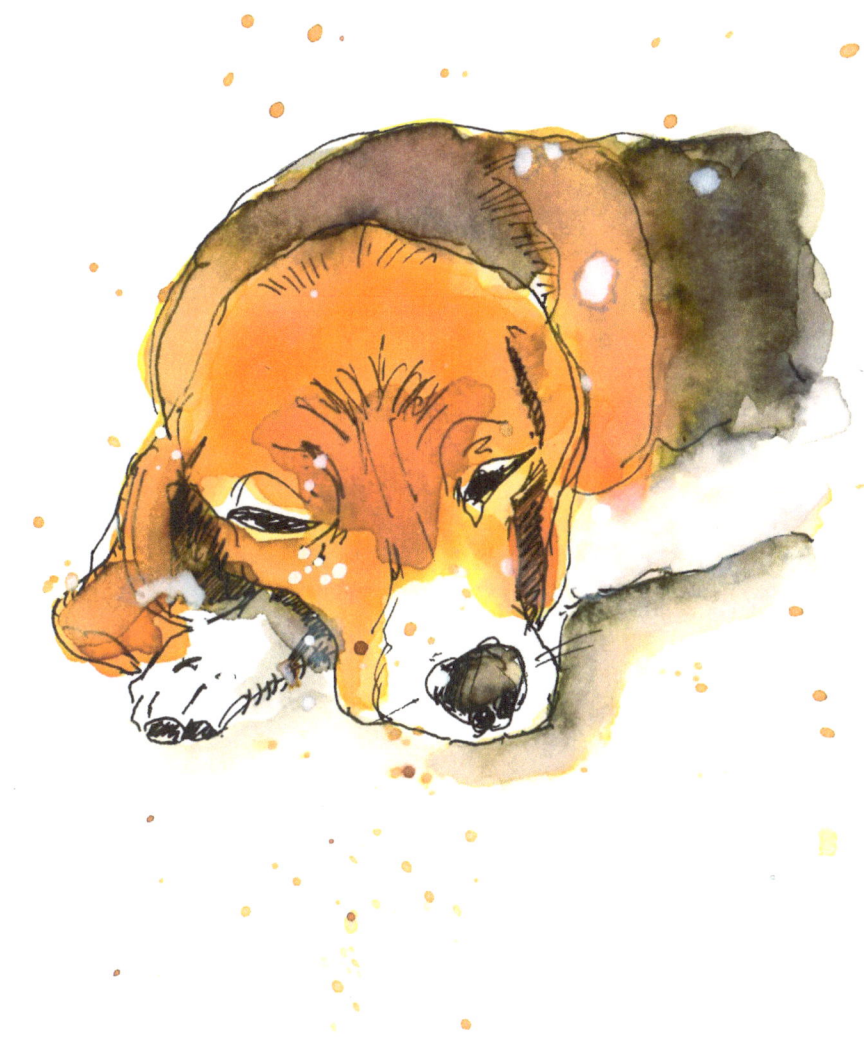

Abby

London, England

Abby, a cute Basset hound, was picked up as a stray wandering the streets of East London. Untagged and unchipped, Abby was soon put on the at-risk list after developing a bad case of kennel cough. An SOS went out on social media desperately looking for the owner before it was too late. Abby's parents were never located, but Marjorie arrived in the nick-of-time to save Abby from a very uncertain future. It's tough enough being in a shelter, but even harder for a sick dog.

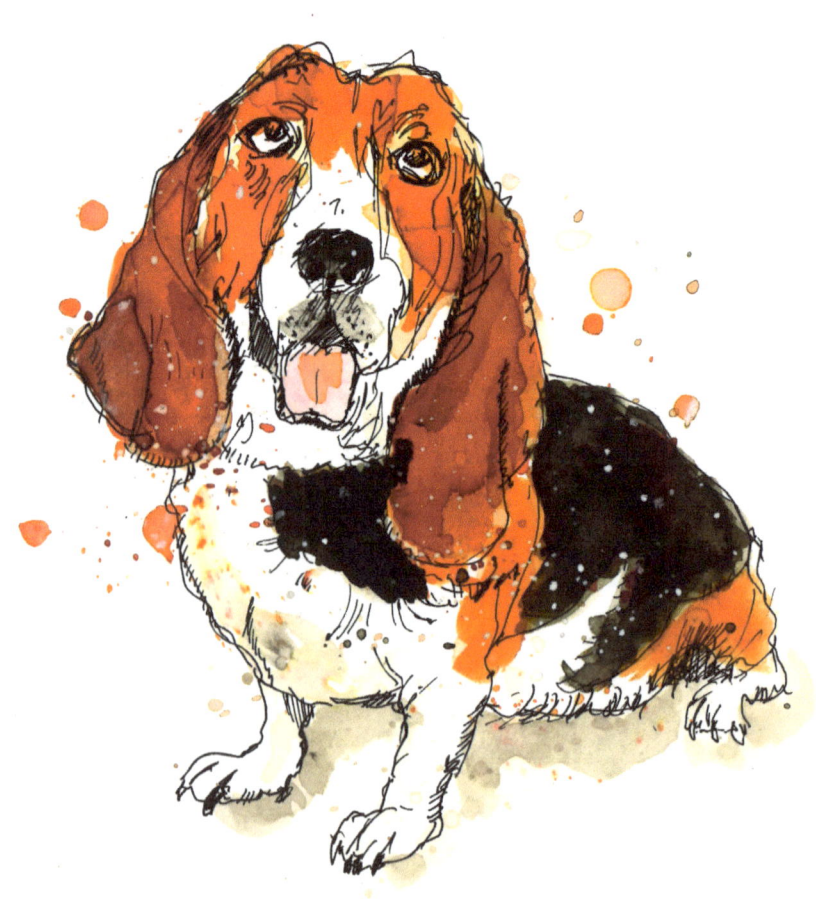

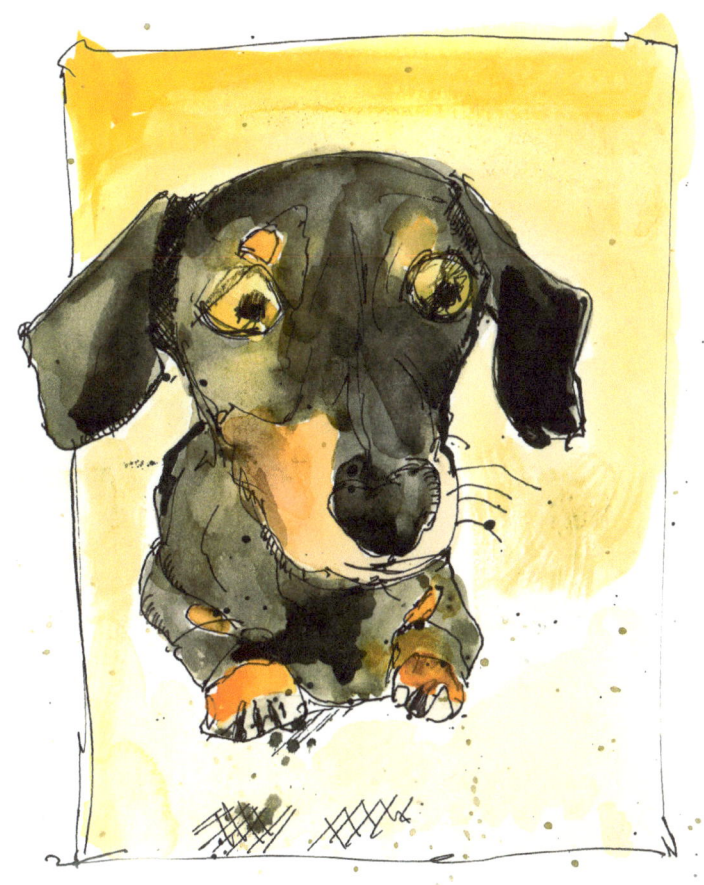

Harry

Dubbo, Australia

Poor Harry! Three homes in three weeks! Harry was a victim of his own exuberance - he just couldn't stop barking during the night. After being returned to his Sydney shelter for the second time, arrangements were made to transport this mighty loud mouth to a shelter in country New South Wales. Some clever work from the local staff resulted in Harry finding a loving home on an isolated farm, where he can now bark all night to his heart's content.

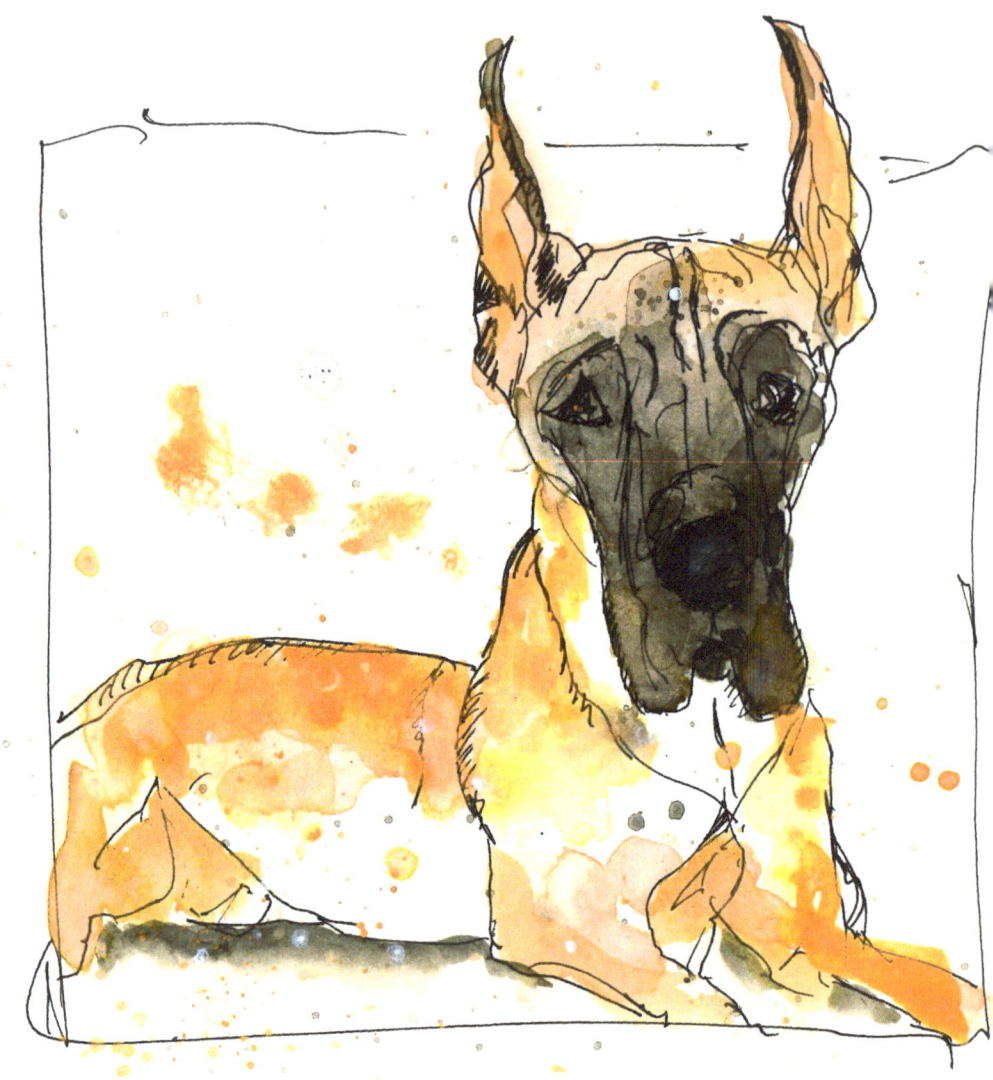

Harley

San Diego, California, USA

Not much is known about Harley's background. He arrived at a San Diego shelter very skinny and very skittish. Obviously he had lived a life of abuse and neglect. When he was rescued by Janet and Martin he had to be carried out to the car - he was even too weak for his freedom walk. Fast-forward 6 months, and after some intense loving care, Harley is well on the way to becoming the confident and loyal pup he was born to be.

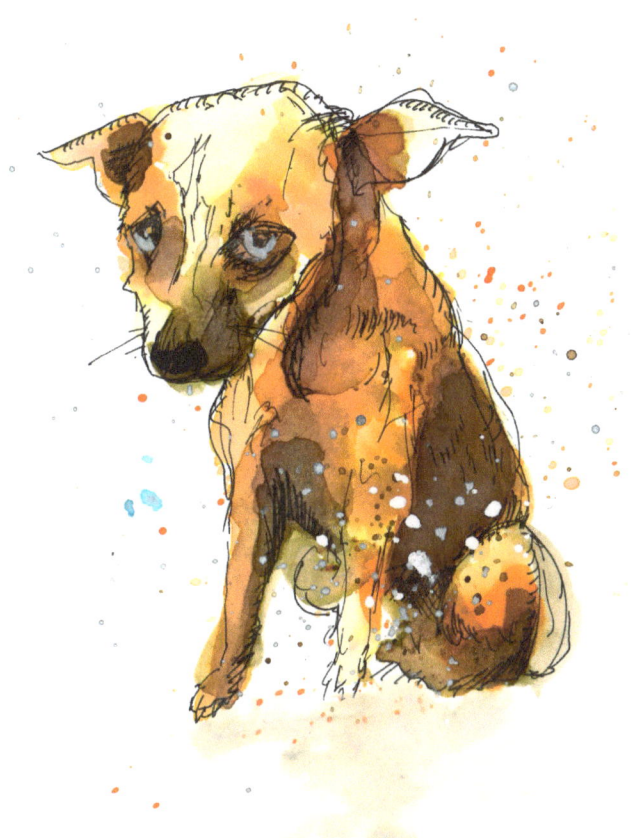

Ruby

San Francisco, California, USA

This sad little girl is Ruby. Spotted at the back of her cage by rescuer Greg, Ruby was almost invisible amidst the throng of jumping, barking dogs, all desperate for some human attention. Ruby was the lucky one that day, and is now safe and secure in her new home. She is possibly looking sad because of all her friends left behind.

Frederick

Surrey, England

A royal name for a royal dog. Formally known as Rex (people still name their dog Rex?) Frederick started a new life seven years ago with James and Helen. Chasing birds in his huge garden is now the highlight of Fred's day.

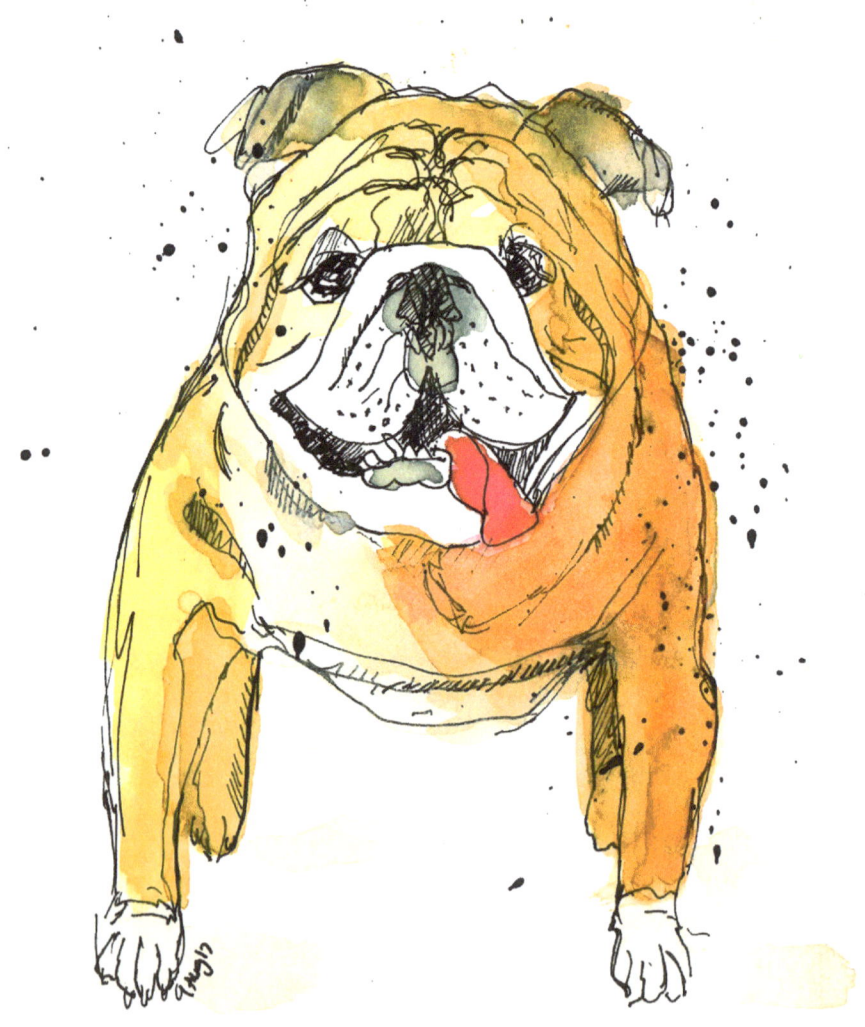

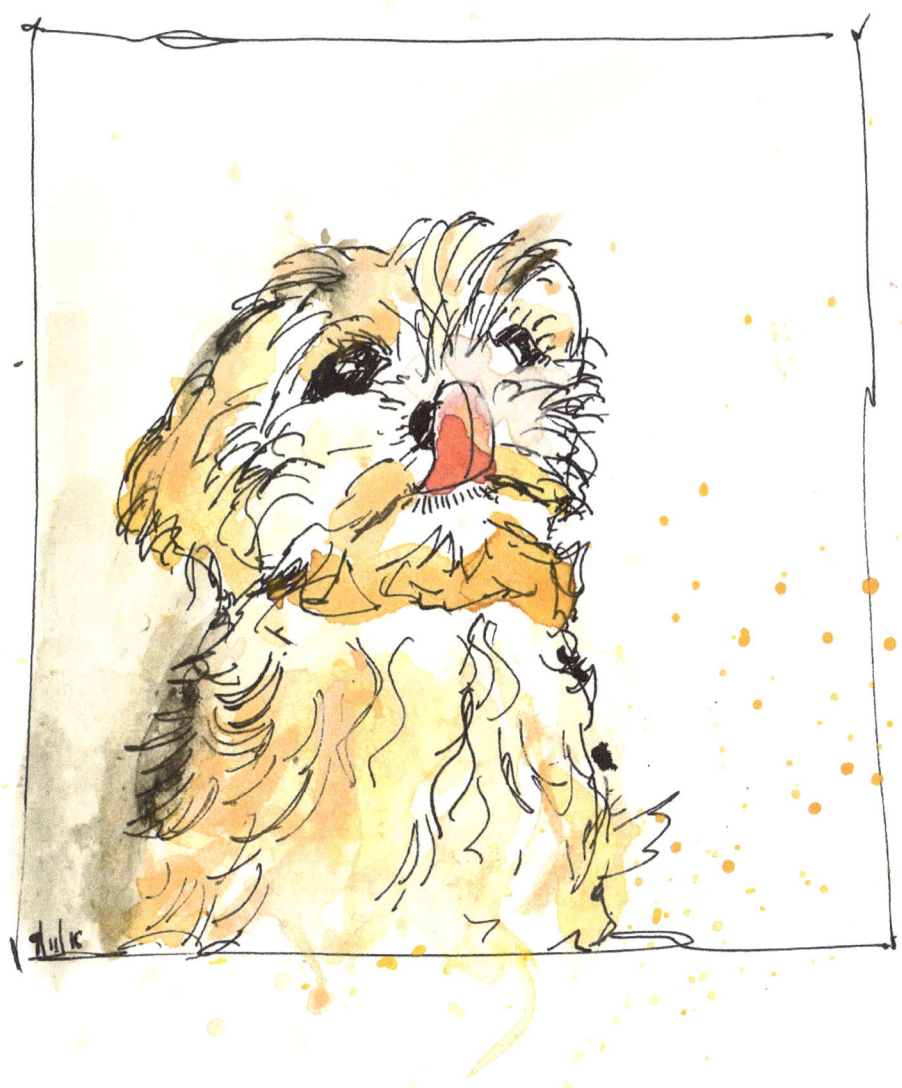

Ceaser

Canberra, Australia

Who could resist this happy friendly face? Not Jane and Marcus, that's for sure. Another successful rescue! Ceaser, a little terrier mix was rescued within days of landing himself in an ACT shelter. Obviously, he got lucky. So many dogs, just as cute as Ceaser, spend *months* waiting for their forever family to come along. So even if you aren't in a position to adopt, there are lots of opportunities for volunteering!

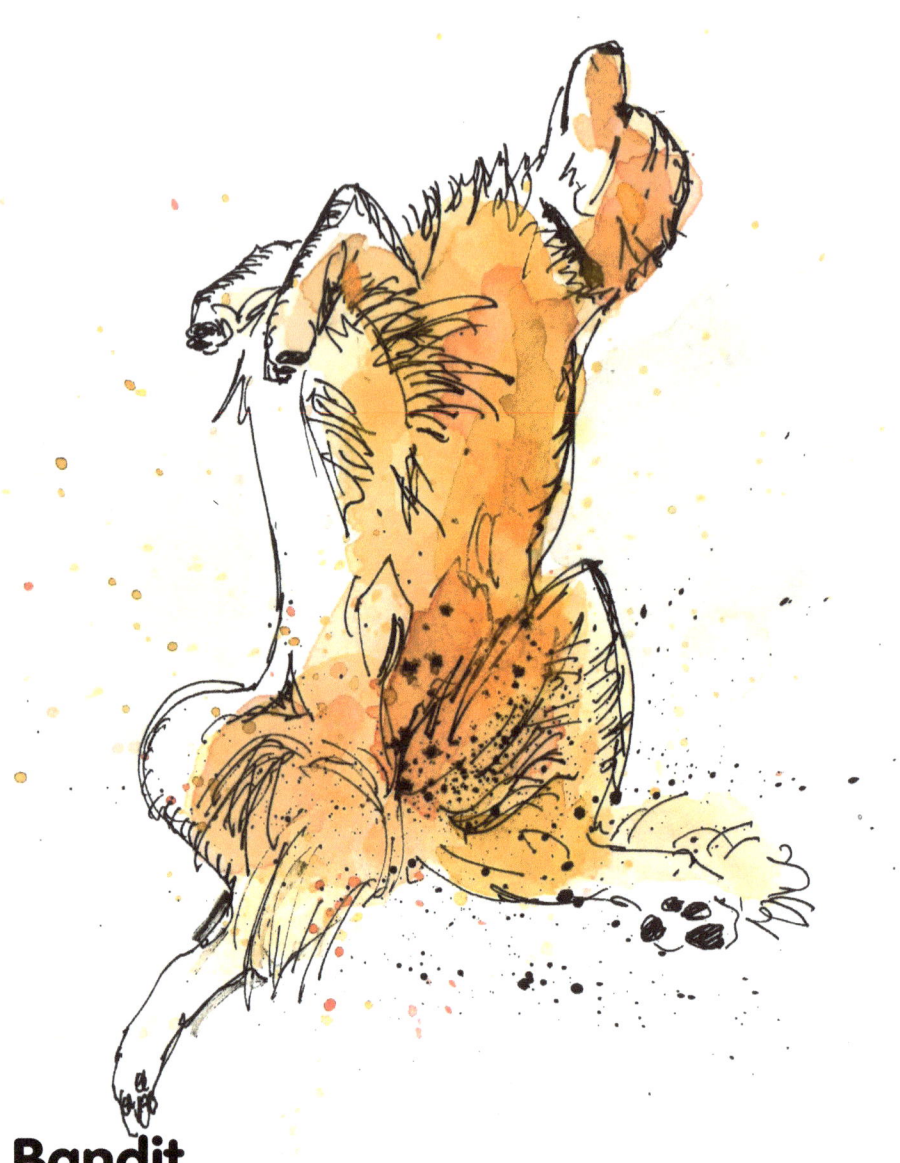

Bandit

Austin, Texas, USA

Bandit was saved by a local Austin rescuer. He had been the runt of the litter and was tossed out of the birthing box by his own mother. Sad, but that's Nature for you. In the loving and sympathetic care of Diane (who incidentally had rescued his mother prior to her giving birth), he had to be hand fed until old enough to fend for himself. Now he won't stop eating.

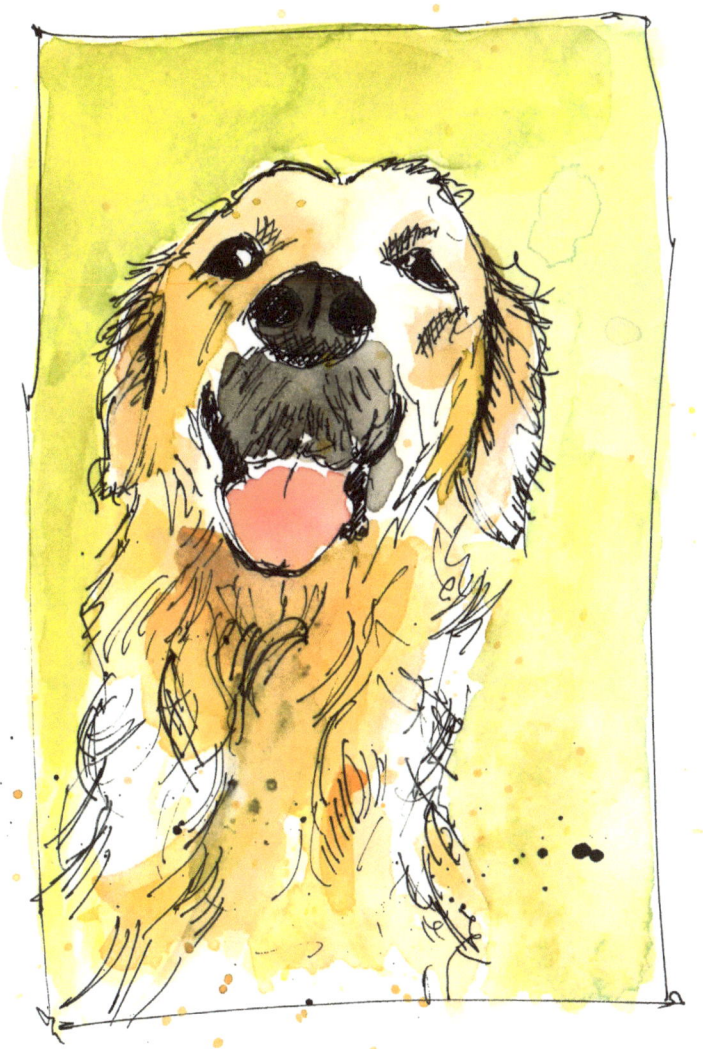

Basil

Sydney, Australia

Our first Goldie! Young Basil here won the pup jackpot when he landed himself in the loving home of Andy and Jac, and now (human!) sibling, Abigail. A true water baby, Basil is truly living the life every dog deserves, and returning the favour by displaying constantly his loving, child-like personality. A match made in heaven. There's a pup for everyone if you know where to look!

Ribot

Auckland, New Zealand

Another Chihuahua mix with a chequered history. And another microchip where the owner was contacted but not the slightest bit interested in coming to the shelter to collect. A blessing for young Ribot. If an owner is not prepared to walk over broken glass to collect their dog – said dog is better off without them. A new, and infinitely better life was awaiting this dynamo pup in the home of Jess and Tommy P!

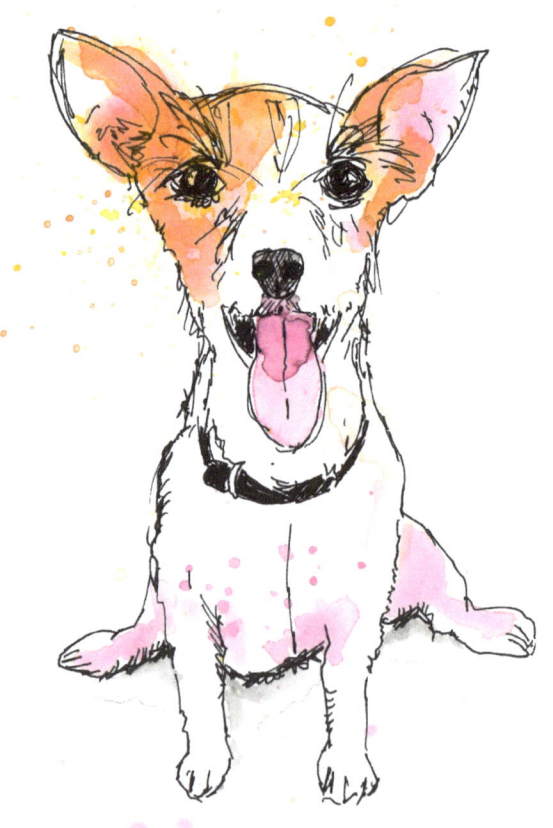

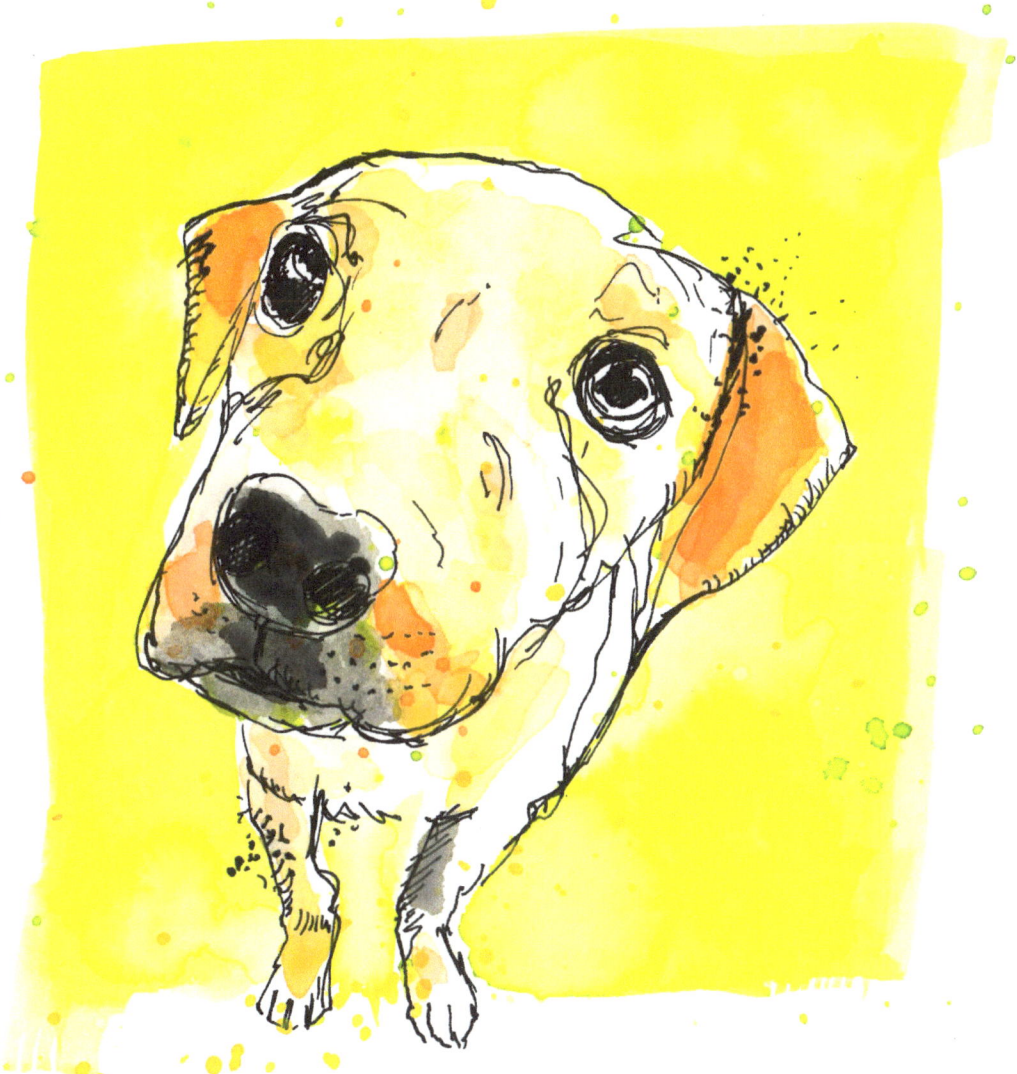

Lacey

Lincoln City, Oregon, USA

Lacey was saved from certain death by animal lovers Brian and Ann.
Lacey was deaf, and had a history of aggression toward other animals, near-constant
"fly-snapping" behaviour, and severe anxiety, resulting in pacing, repetitive pouncing
and yelping. It took 6 years of VERY patient love and care, and special behavioural
training but now Lacey is well and truly a reformed pup. Special-need dogs need
homes too.

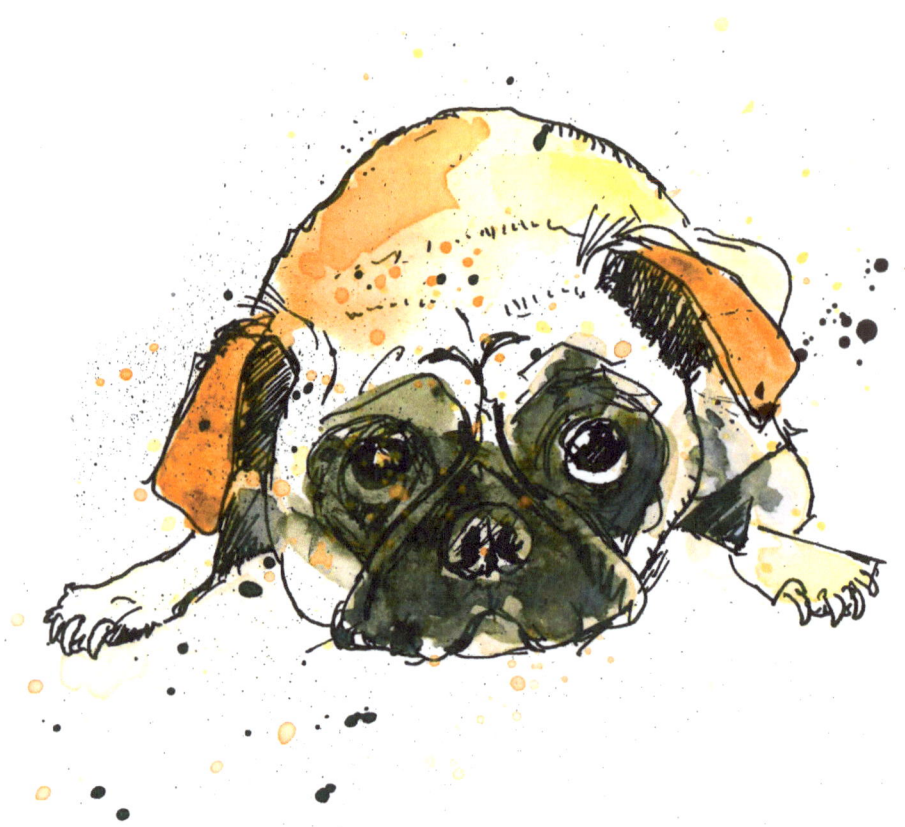

Ted

Alberta, Canada

No one is quite sure of Ted's back-story. He was found literally wandering the streets, tired and hungry, with no microchip. Fernando, the big softie that he is, gave him the loving home he deserves, and he has no regrets despite little Ted's penchant for destroying shoes! A happy story in the end, but perhaps sad for the original owners, but for the sake of a microchip, will never know what happened to their little Teddy.

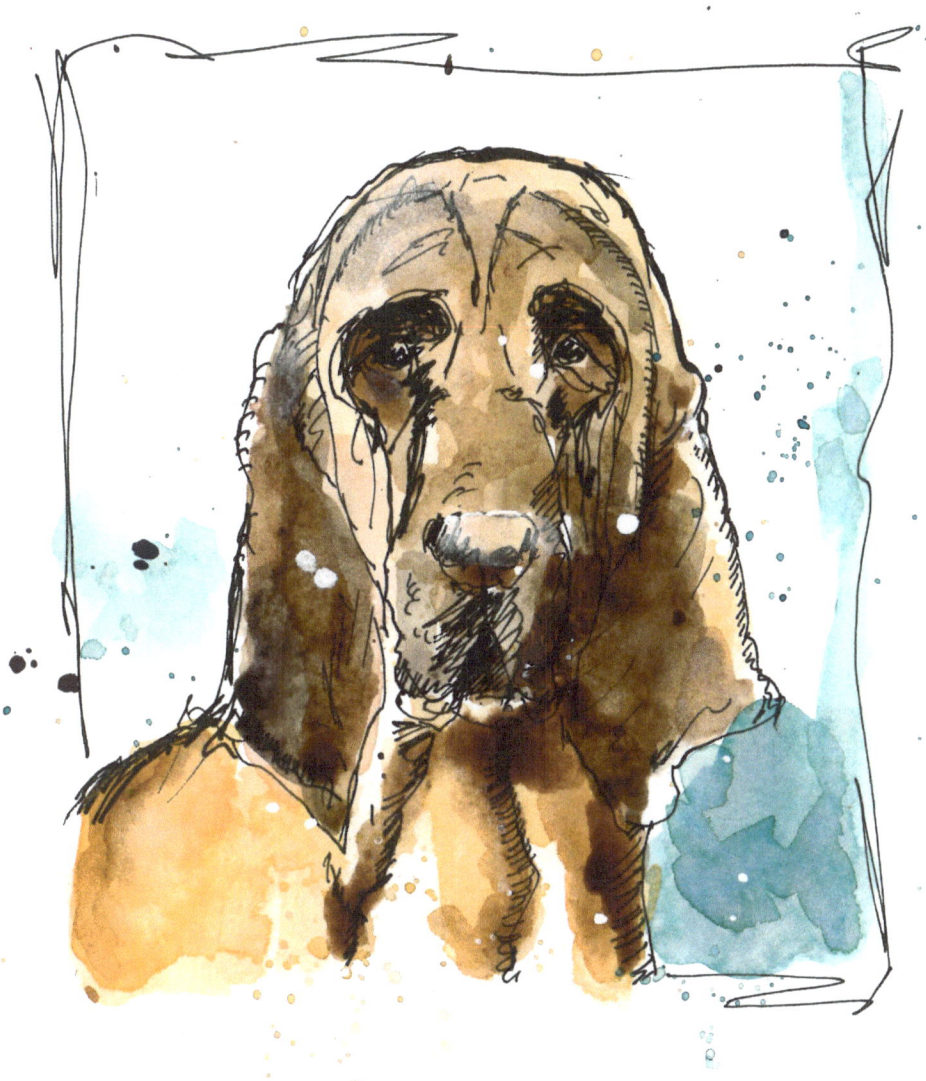

Big Max

New York, NY, USA

Another pound dog, dumped by his owners because they were moving. A familiar story the world over. If you're going to abandon a member of the family, do you have to do it at a high-kill facility?? Big Max, should be renamed Lucky Max, because two saints, named Angela and Charles stepped in, and now Big Max is back where belongs – at home slobbering all over the furniture.

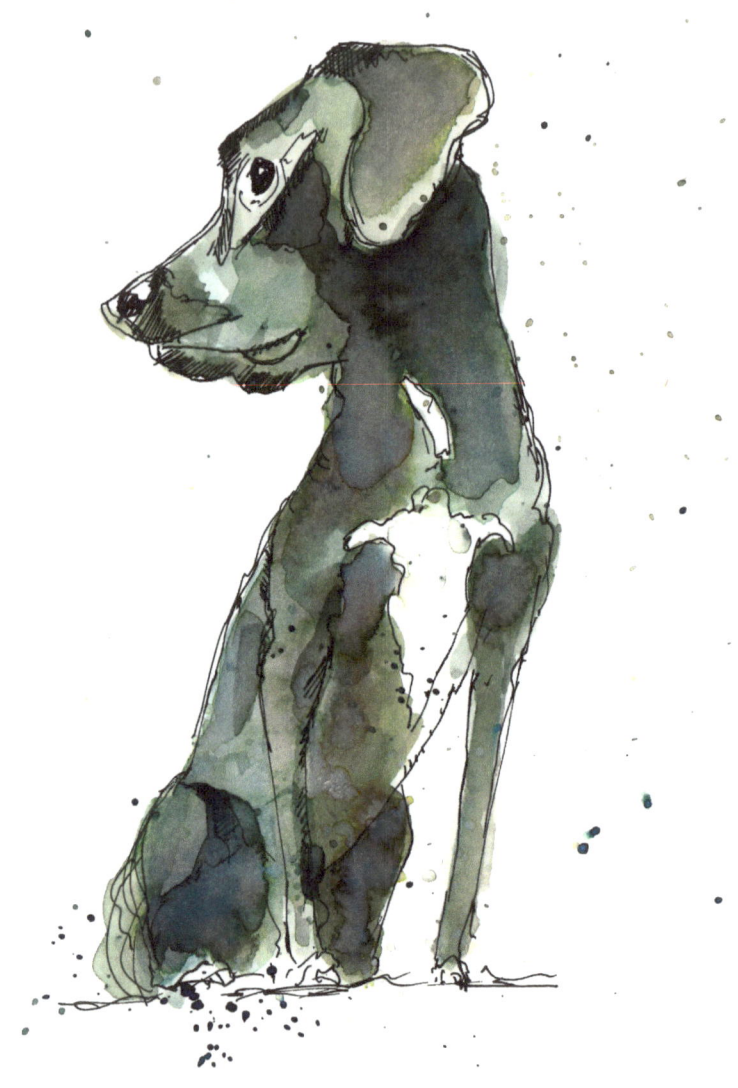

Silverpaw

Tegernsee, Germany

Meet Silverpaw. Starved, wounded and near death, his days were numbered. Until he was lucky enough to fall into the loving care of Mona. Surgery, medicine, healthy food, and a bucketful of love and care, have completely transformed Silverpaw into the bright happy and healthy dog he is today. Mona and her family – more wonderful examples of why you should adopt, not shop!

Jezzabelle and Maggie

Sydney, Australia

Just another two pups livin' the dream. 10-year-old Jezzabelle (the big one) is the apple of the eye of young Maggie May (the little one). The pair were made for each other, and receive bucketloads of love and attention from their mum Debra, a dog lover of the highest order. Deb makes sure her youngsters want for nothing, and they live the dog's life they richly deserve.

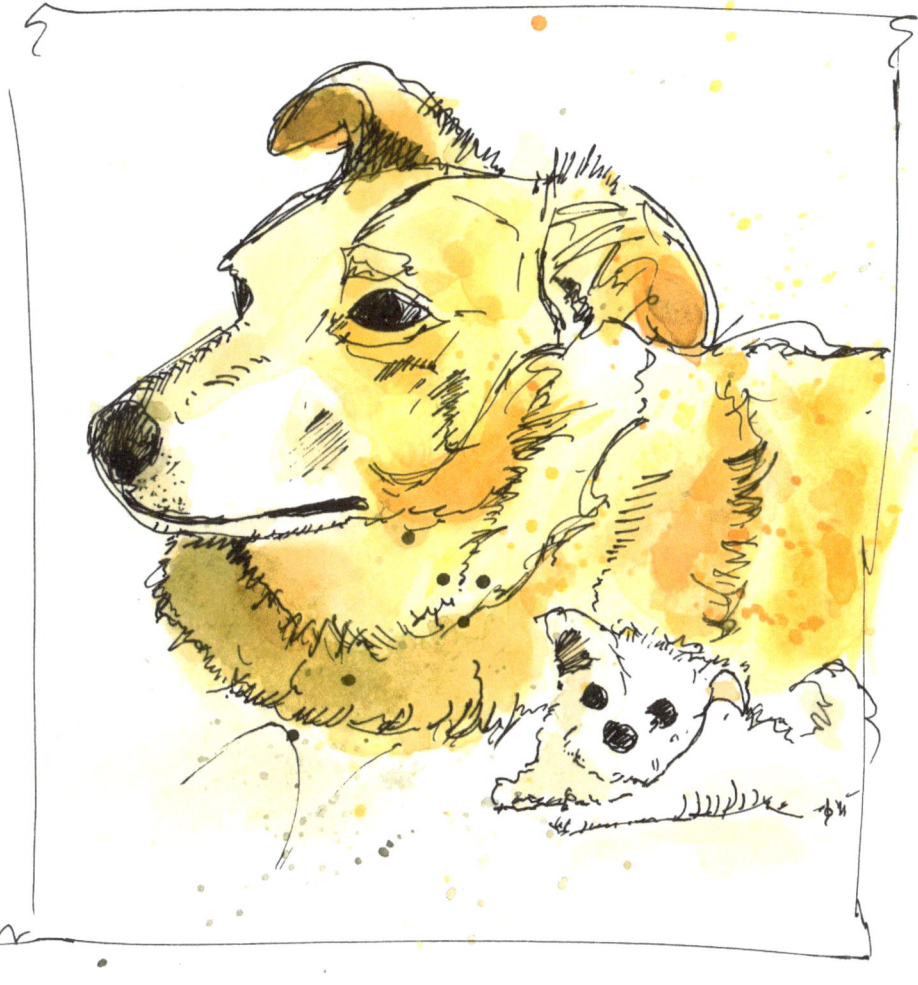

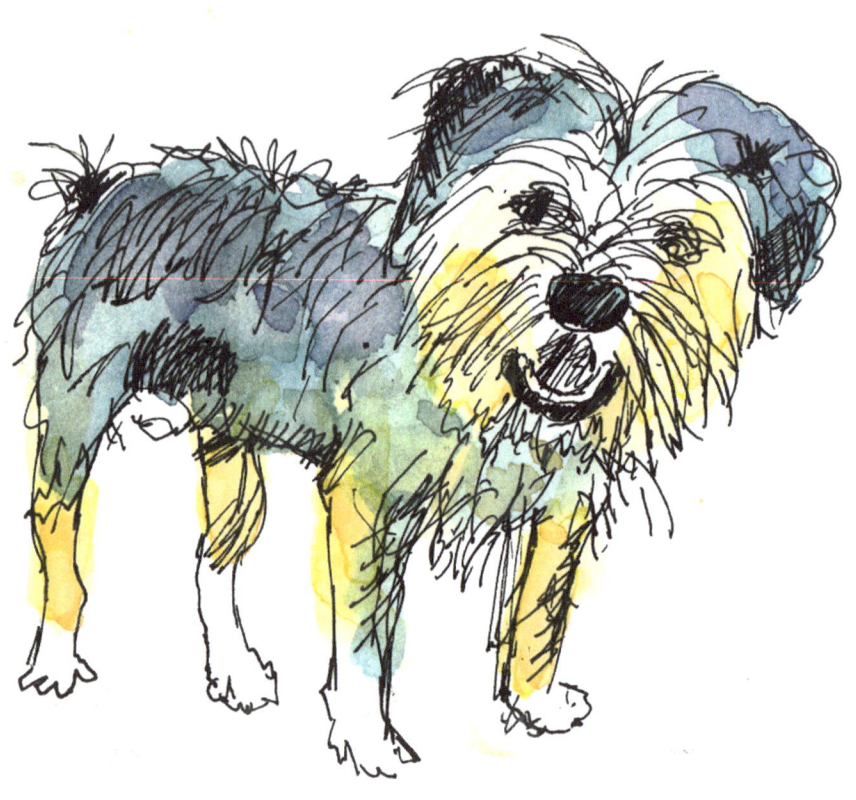

Rinley

Jackson, Mississippi, USA

Puppy mills - the scourge of the pet world! Poor Rinley arrived at the shelter in a cardboard box sealed with duct tape. Upon opening it, shelter staff discovered a poor, terrified pup weighing only 5 pounds, even with all the mats that covered her body, including her eyes. The staff were at least thankful the pitiful owner hadn't just euthanised her and at least given her a slight chance at a new beginning.

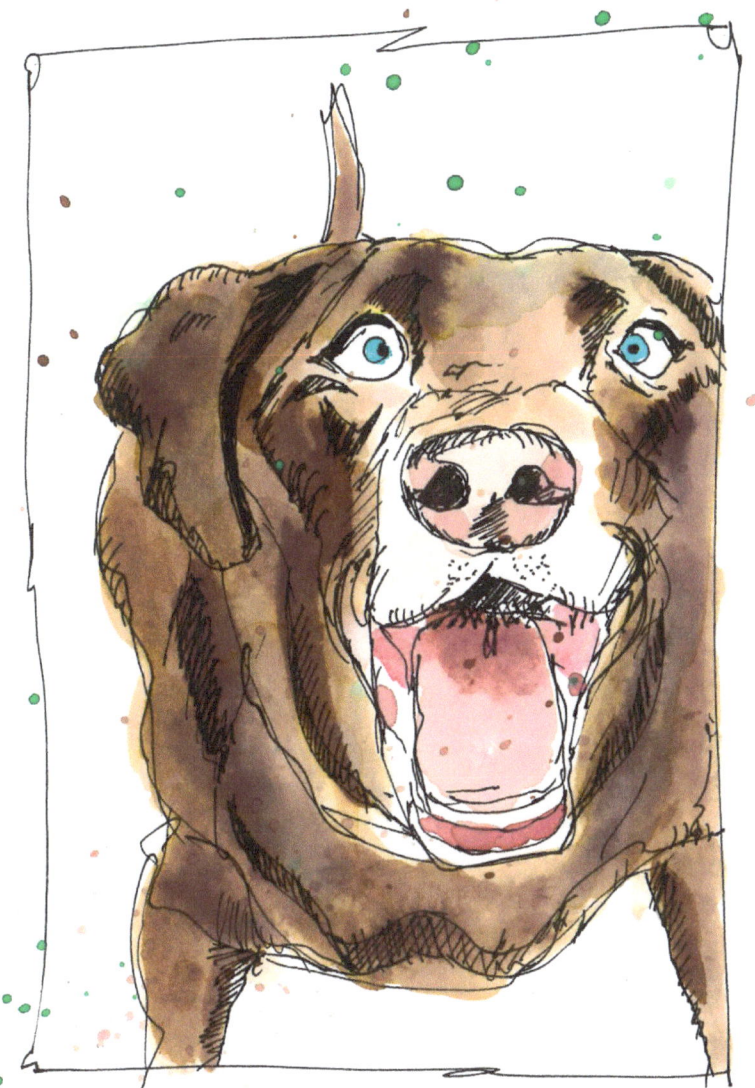

Zilker

Longmont, Colorado, USA

Zilker! AKA 'The Monster'. AKA 'Z-Monster'. AKA 'Zee'. Another pup with a rough start
in life, he was abandoned in a Walmart carpark and taken in by the kind folks at
Safe Harbor Lab Rescue in Golden, Colorado. But who in their right mind was going
to adopt this 95-pound wrecking ball? Alisa, slightly crazy enough, and certainly
big-hearted enough, stood up and the pair have never looked back!

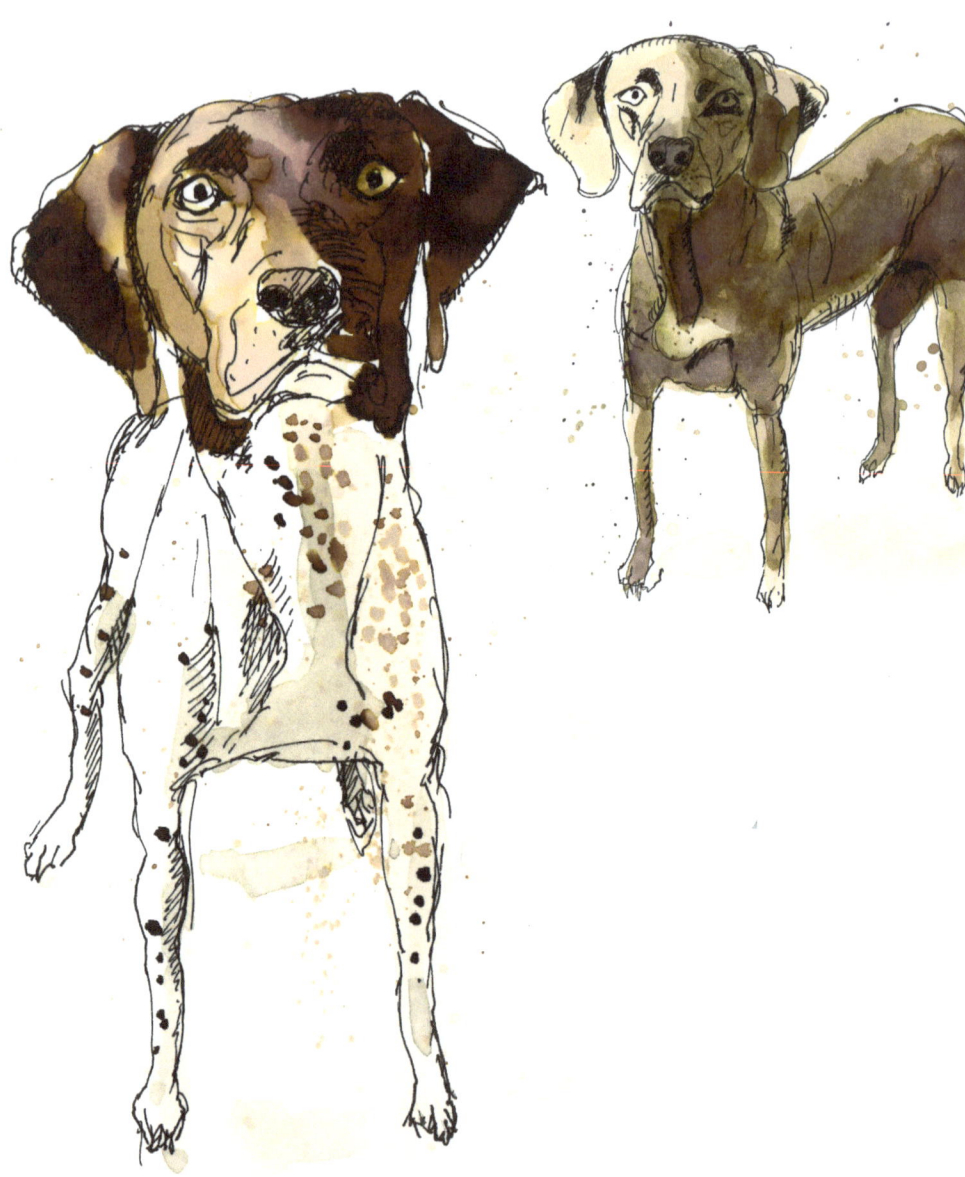

Hattie and Finley

Prosper, Texas, USA

Meet Finley and Hattie! Two long-stridin', attitude-wielding, but completely adorable Texans! Finn and Hattie didn't exactly have the best start in life. Finn, abused and neglected at the hands of humans who simply had no right to be anywhere near another living creature and Hattie, a cancer-survivor. Their lives both changed dramatically when they came under the care of Julie. After a skittish and withdrawn start, both pups are beginning to bloom and living the life of happiness, nurturing, love and discipline they both craved.

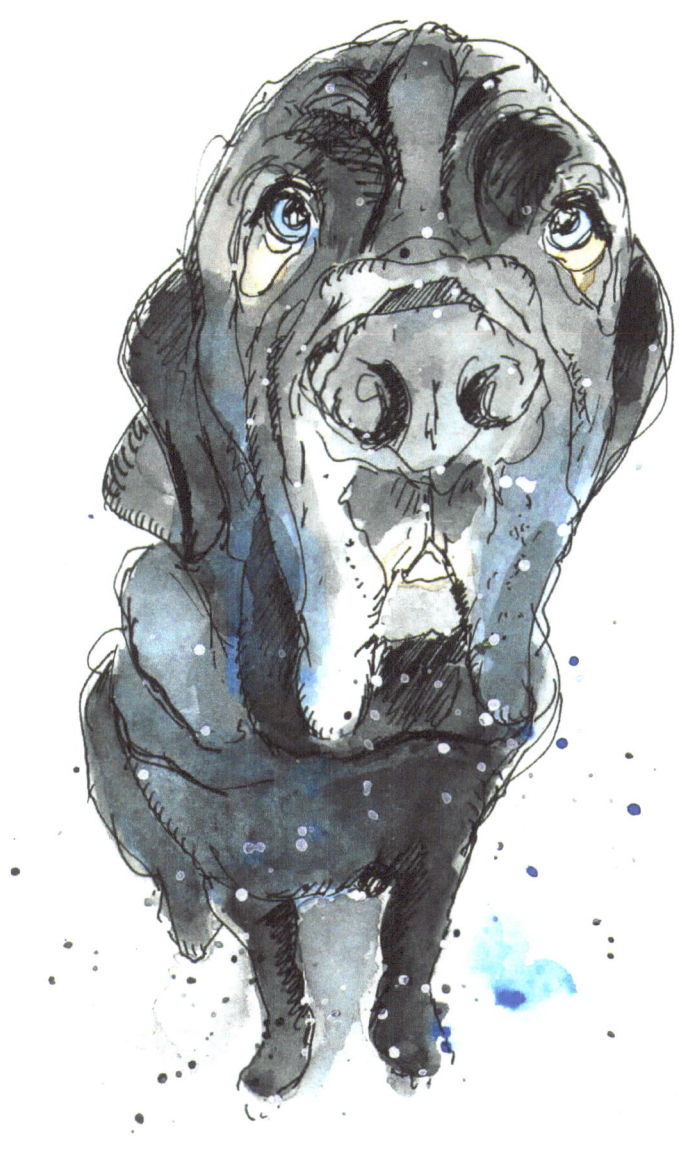

Stark

Arvada, Colorado, USA

Stark here, with the stunning white patch on his chest (just like his namesake Ironman!), came into Mikaila's life on her 16th birthday. They instantly became best friends and went everywhere together. Sadly this happy and cuddly neopolitan mastiff passed away from cancer just weeks before his 4th birthday. A short life certainly, but living the outdoor Colorado lifestyle with Mikaila, he made every minute count.

Walter

Sydney, Australia

Meet Walter! Young Wally here was destined for a (probably short) life of misery and wire cages at a Sydney shelter. Thankfully he was rescued and is now happily ensconced with the Peaty family (as if it wasn't chaotic enough already) and human siblings Mitchell and Hannah. Another success story, kudos to the Peaty's for opening their home, and choosing to adopt and not shop.

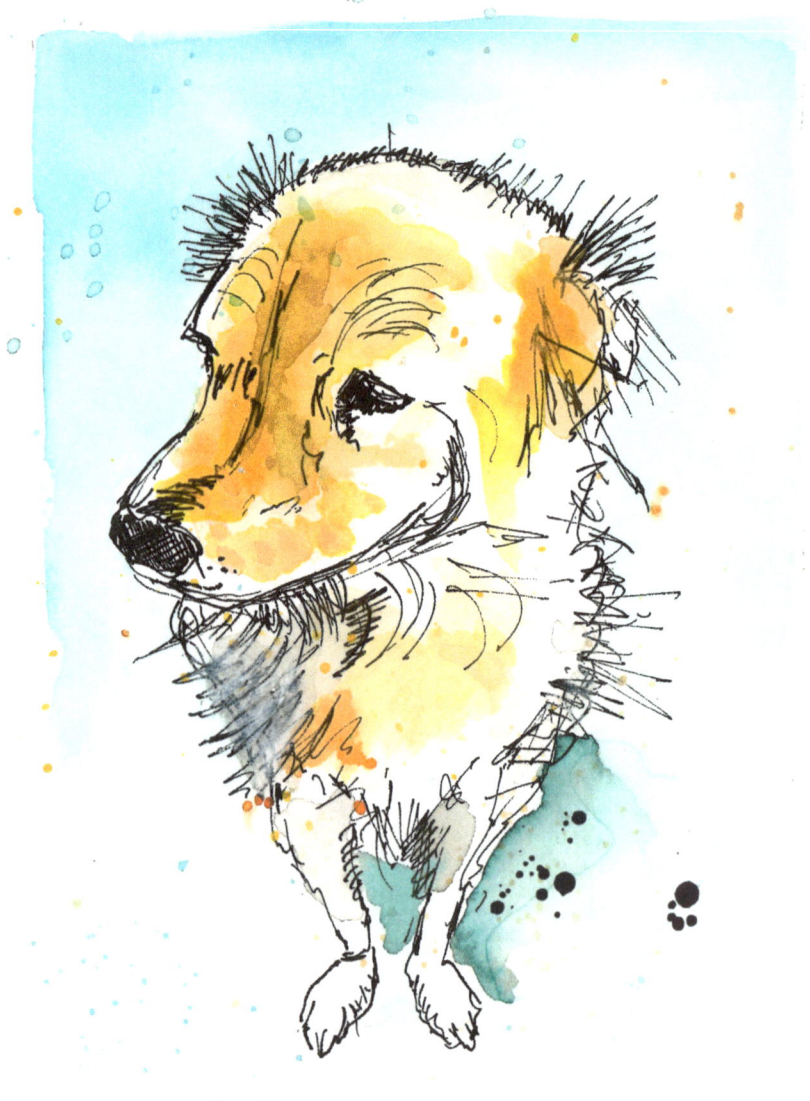

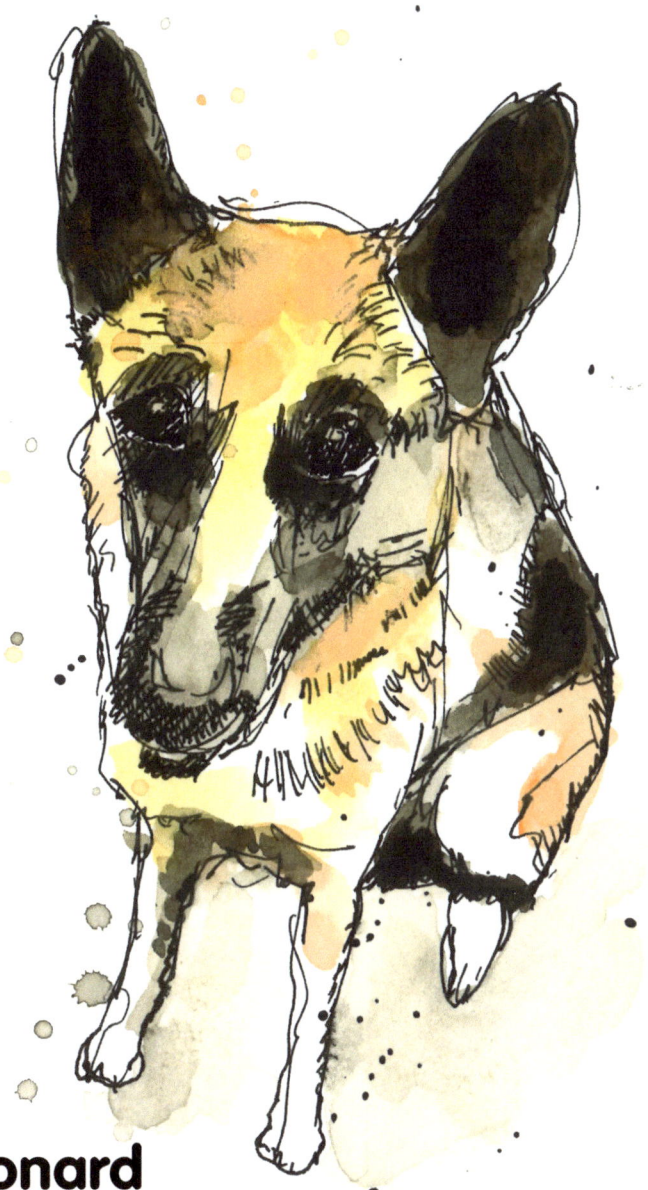

Leonard

San Francisco, California, USA

Let's hear it for foster parents! A vital cog in the rescue dog operation. Leonard, brought in as a stray, had several wounds and injuries from being attacked by another dog. He spent days in the shelter, but was quickly earmarked for the needle as no one was interested in a wounded dog. Enter our heroes, Katie and Bill, plucking Leonard form harm's way, and allowing him time to recuperate before looking for his forever home.

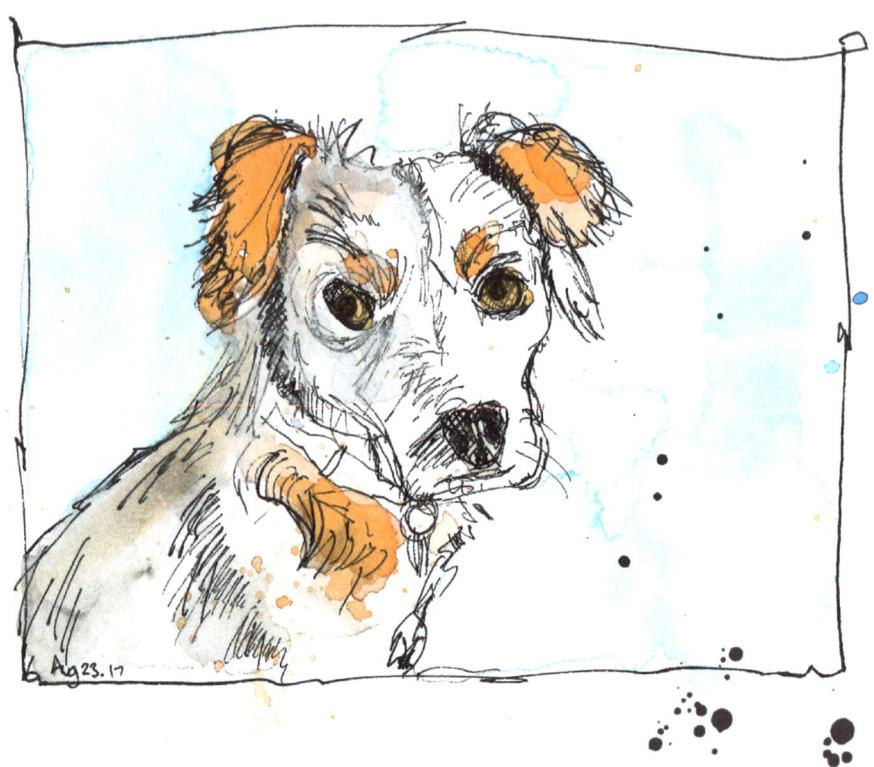

Rufus

Sydney, Australia

This is Rufus from a shelter in Sydney's west. He deserves a better back-story, but sadly no one knows what it is. Adopt, don't shop people!

Mason

Blue Mountains, Australia

Mason is a 2.5 year old Chihuahua, who spends his days as an assistant dog, bringing independence and confidence to his human mum, Kimberley. Is there a greater calling for a family pet? A naturally timid soul, Mason loves his outdoor adventures, chilling with his Jack Russell friend, Gromit, and his human aunt, Kate.

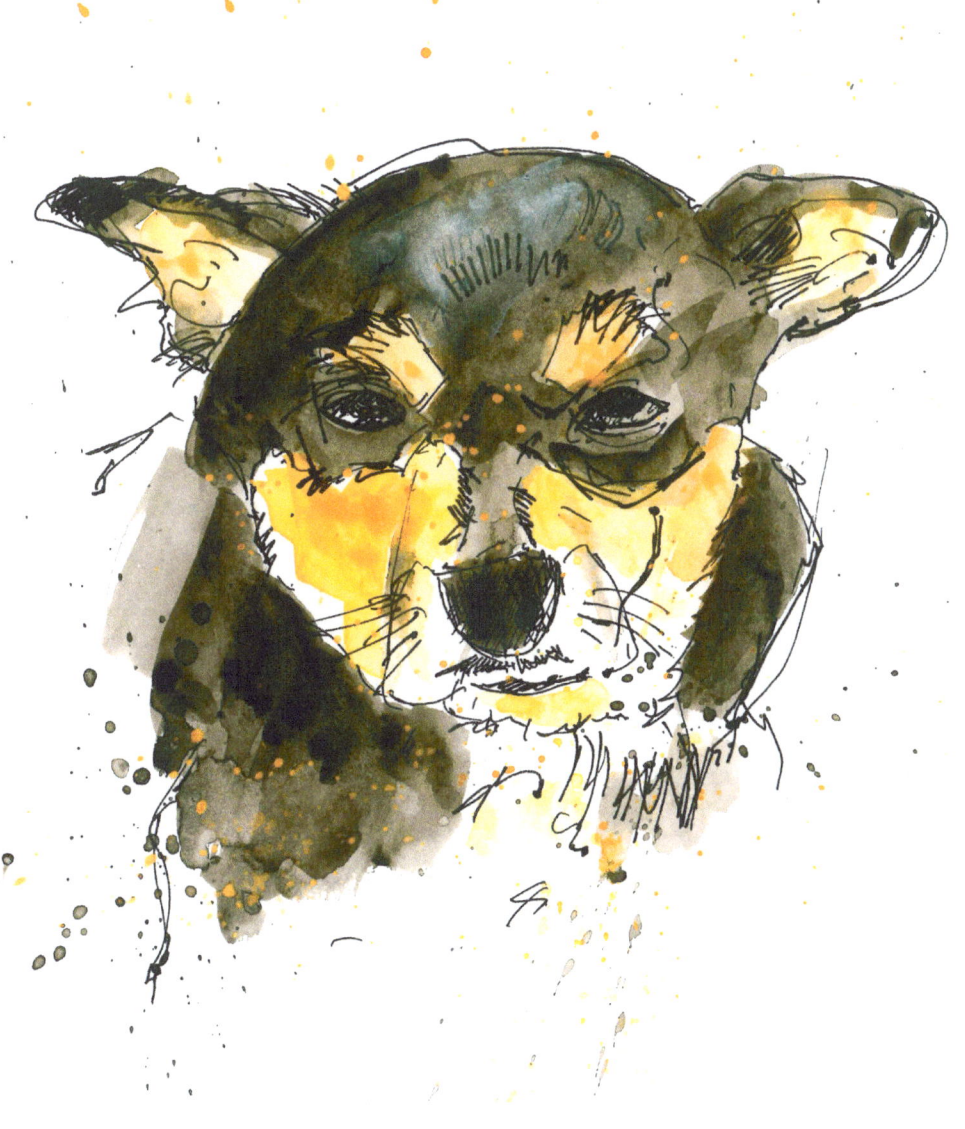

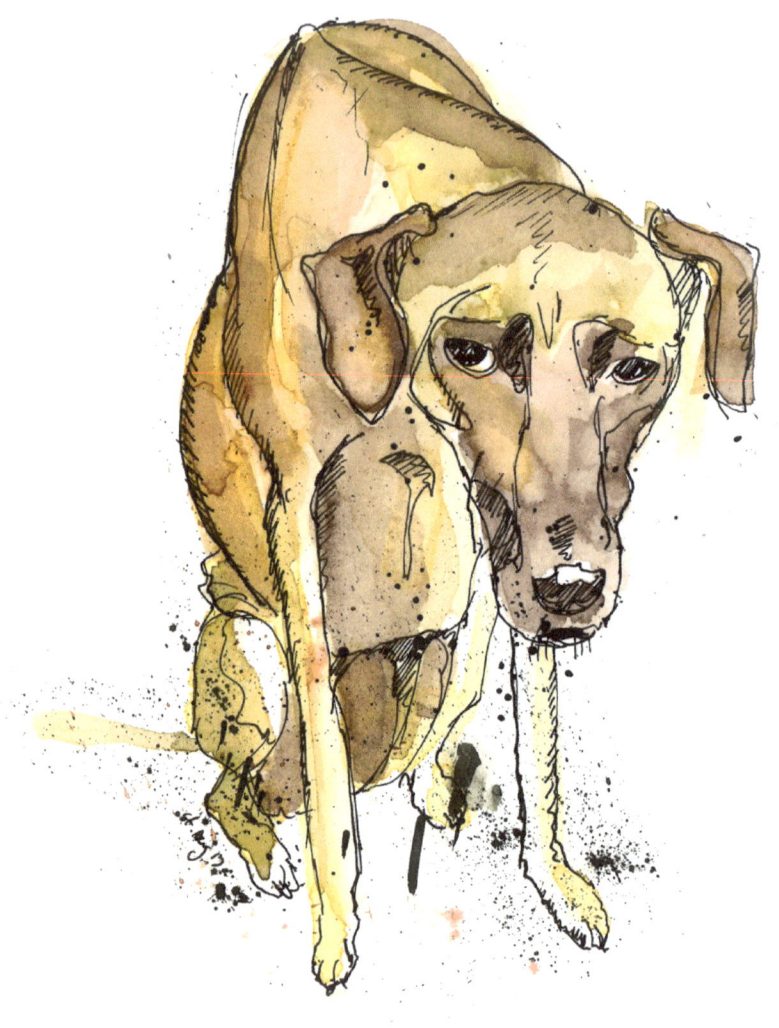

Pegasus

Sydney, Australia

Pegasus is a somewhat sadder story. He was in such a poor, neglected and emaciated condition when he came into a Sydney shelter and was not expected to last more than one or two nights. He picked up a little bit and went into the home care of Justine and Andrew in Sydney's west. Pegasus passed away a short time later, but at least in his final hours he experienced the love and care he had deserved all along.

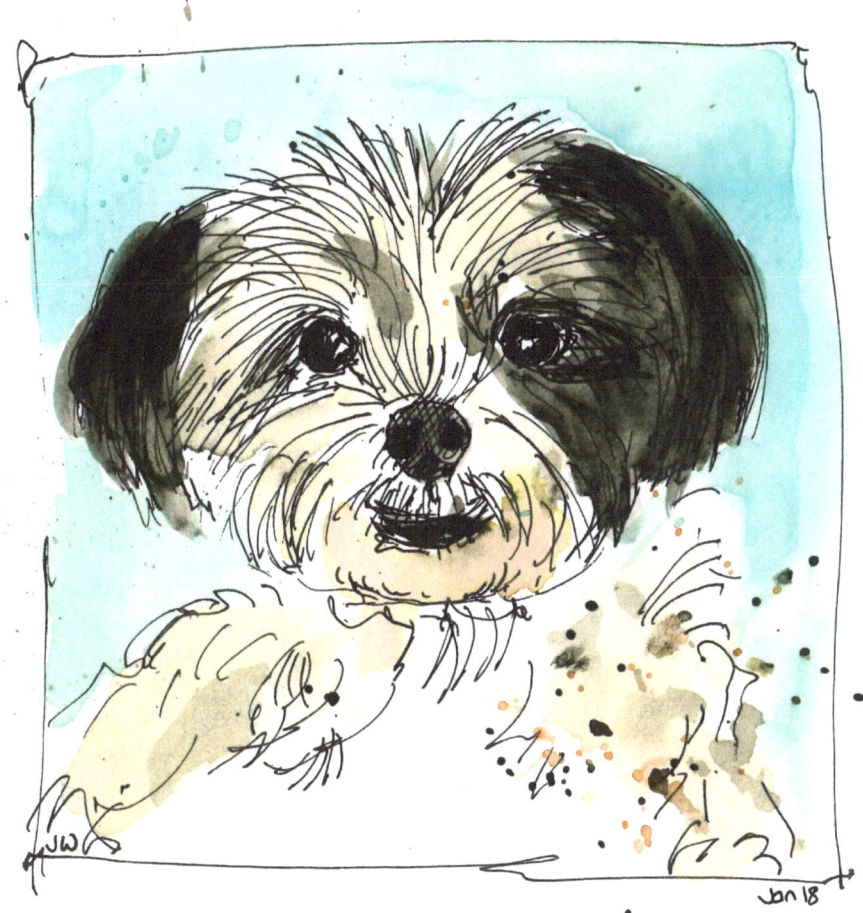

Millie

Sydney, Australia

Sadly no longer with us, little Millie, a Maltese Shih Tzu, lived the life many dogs would envy. Named in honour of the new Millennium, Millie had a wonderful 16 years under the watchful eye of Karen and Peter. Equally at home on land or a boat (but not the wet stuff in between), Millie had no fear, and even had the measure of dogs a lot bigger! When dogs return as much love and joy as they receive, you know something is working right.

Dually

Colorado, USA

This little ball of energy is Dually! Dually lives in Middle-of-Nowhere, Colorado, USA. His sweet mum, Kelli, is an animal lover of the highest order, providing a wonderful home for not only Dually, but his 'siblings' which include an Australian Shepard, two cats, one horse and two longhorns! Of course they all bow to the presence of the mighty Dachshund!

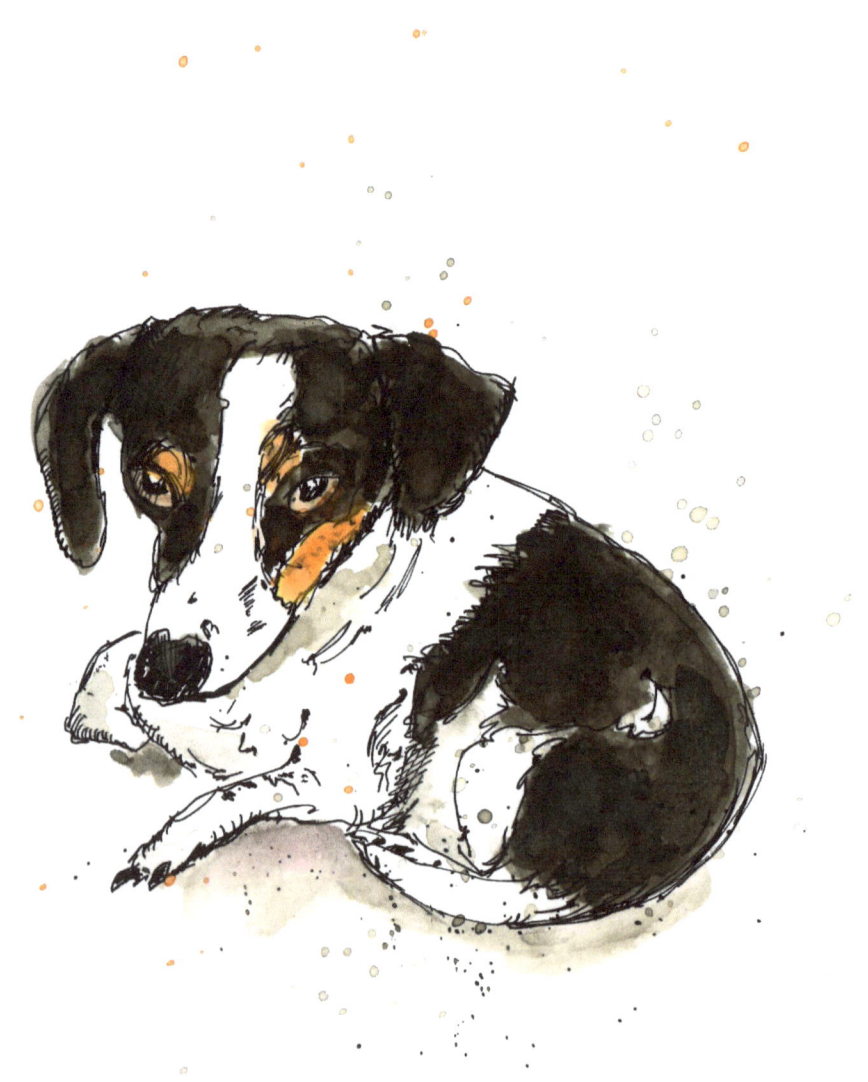

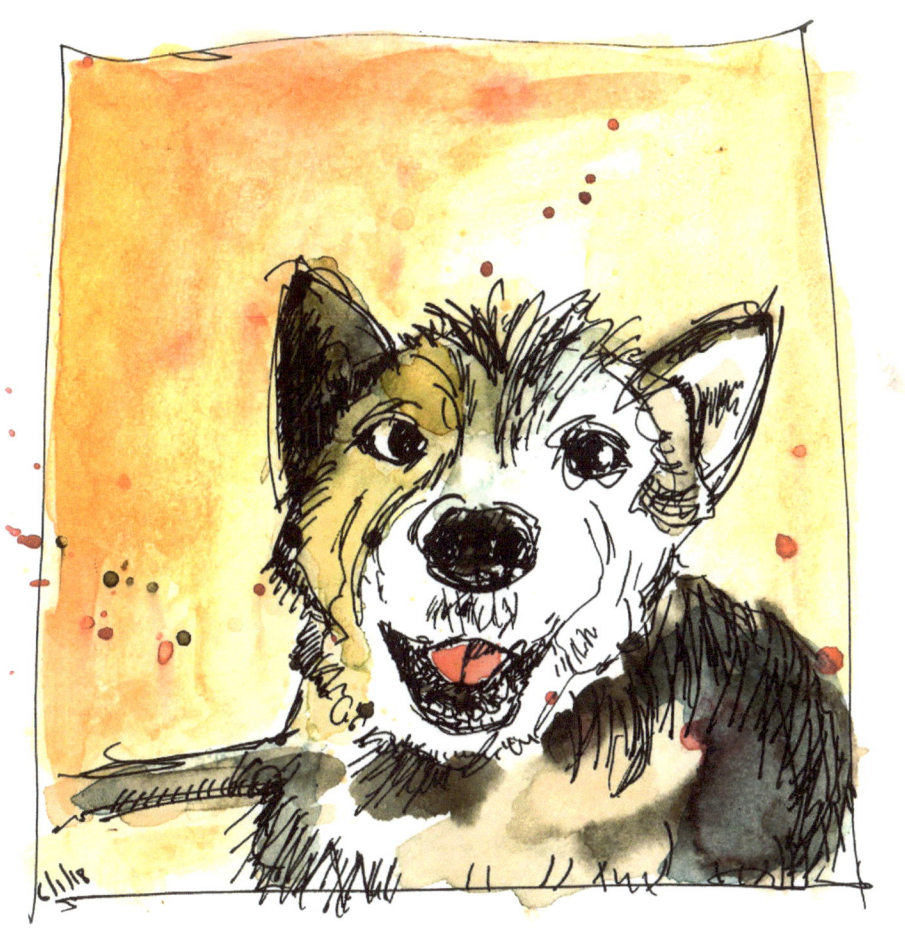

Webster

Brisbane, Australia

Old dogs need loving as well! When 13-year-old Webster's dad suddenly passed away, it looked Webster's days could well be numbered too. A shelter is no place for a senior dog that is set in his ways. Fortunately, neighbours Alice and John stepped in and offered to take care of Webster in his twilight years, saving him from the ignominy of spending his final days alone and frightened.

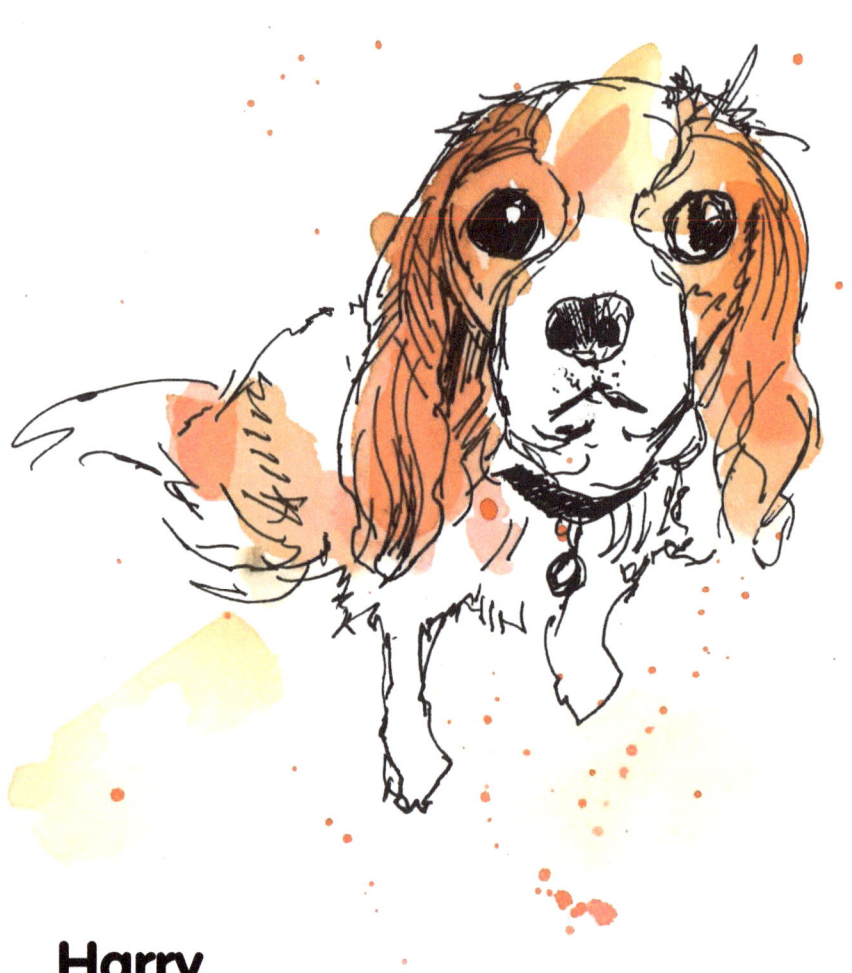

Harry

Ettalong Beach, Australia

Senior dog Harry is just one those dogs that nothing seems to faze. Living the good life on the central coast of NSW, Harry just rolls with the punches and despite some health issues, his mum and dad, Felicity and David, treat him as part of the family. He earns his keep, and often puts more time in at the office than his dad!

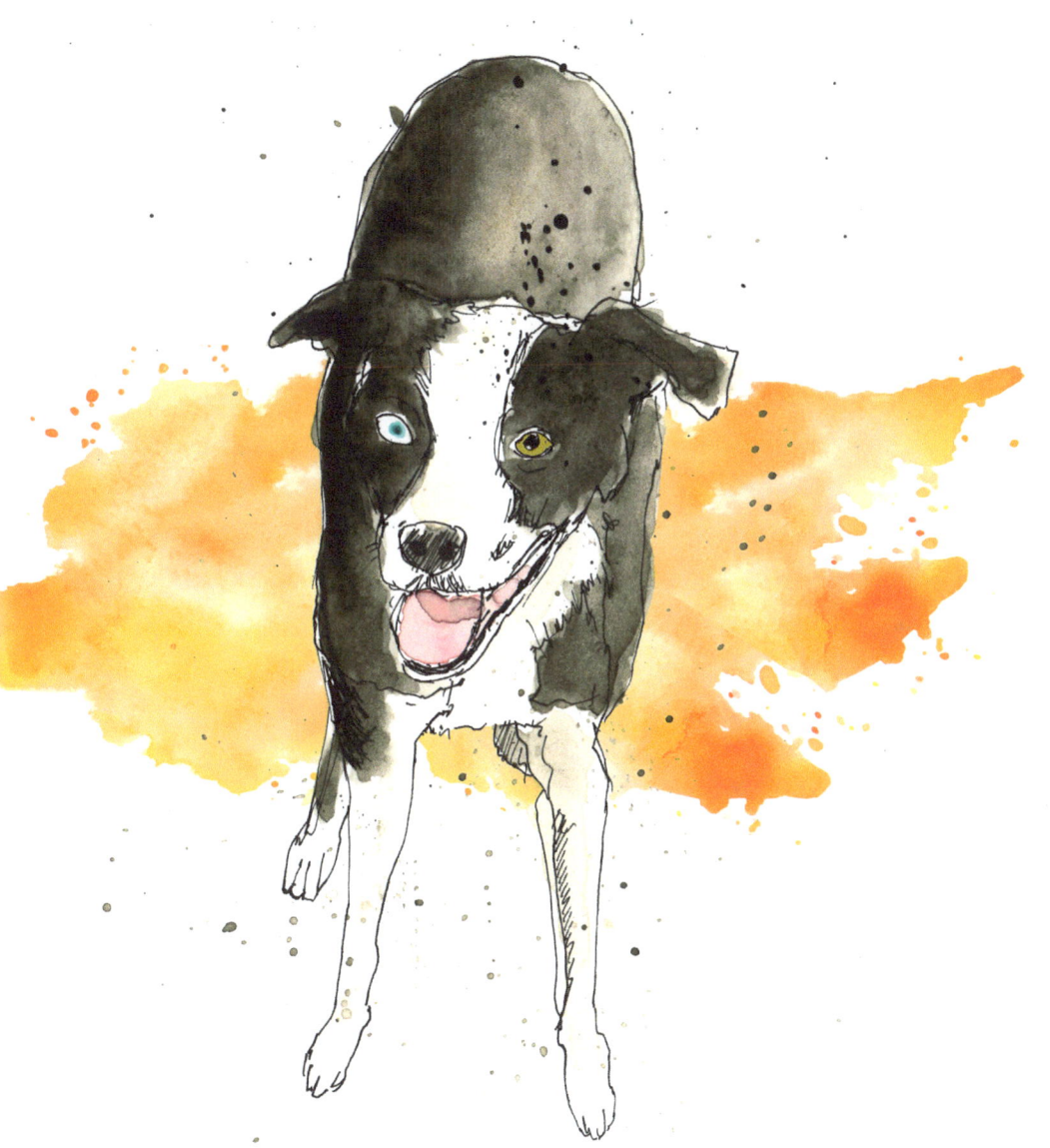

Wiket

Louisville, Colorado, USA

Sometimes rescues happen in reverse. Sometimes it's the human that needs rescuing. Wiket came into Dar's life at a particularly low point, but through Wiket's loving exuberance, things quickly turned around. It wasn't long before Wiks had a human father, Scott and three human siblings, Julian, Avery and Katherine. All the love and support that Wiket had provided in the early years, was then returned ten-fold.

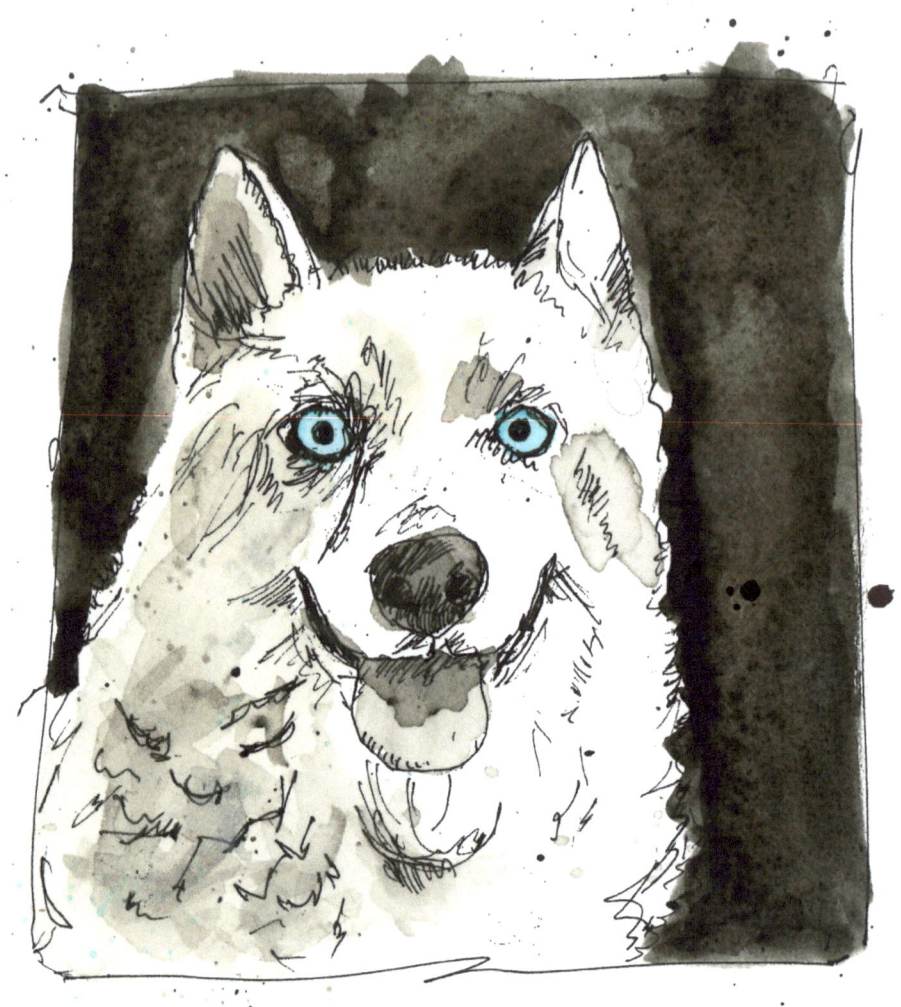

Champion

Sydney, Australia

Champion was only 6 weeks old, scared and alone at the back of her cage, but fortunately caught the eye of a passing Albert, who took her home to a life of safety and love. Human sister Grace appeared on the scene shortly after and the pair were inseparable before Champion's sudden passing in 2016. Truly it was a stroke of luck Albert found her all those years ago, but what a magical life it lead to – for all three of them.

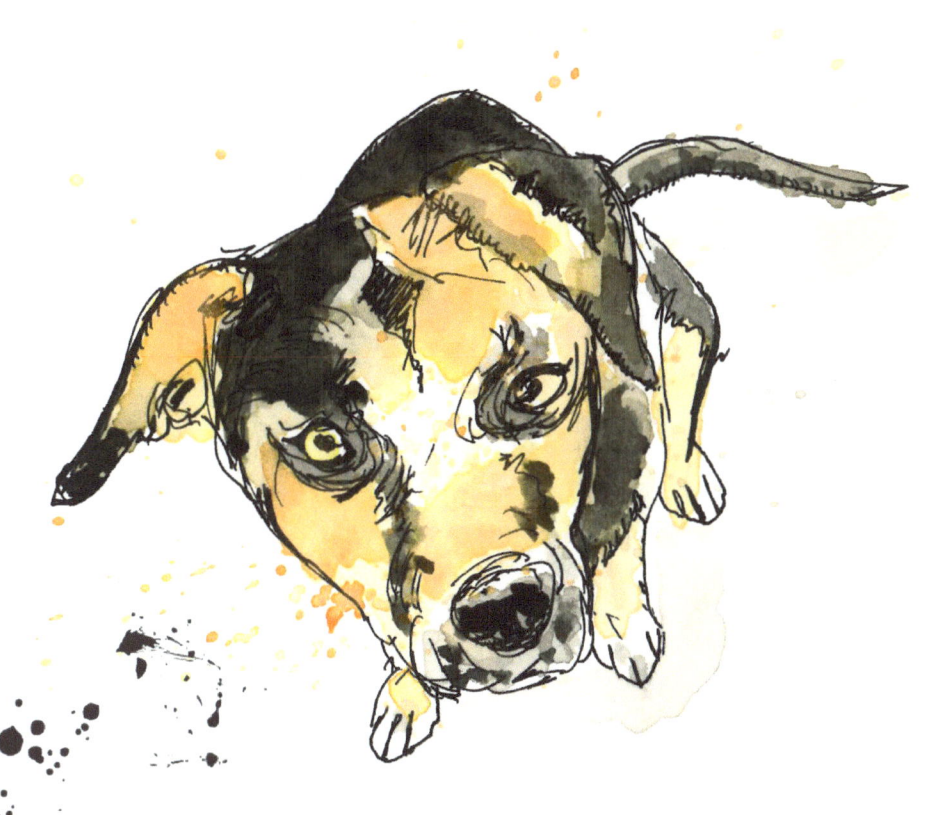

Chewy

Melbourne, Australia

Chewy here was doing it tough. Picked up on the streets of Melbourne he was taken to a shelter with puncture wounds and bruises all over him. It's not easy surviving on the street when you're so small. A good big dog will always beat a good little dog. He is in good hands now, but only through good luck. Next time you see a dog wandering on the street, call someone – you may be saving the life of another Chewy.

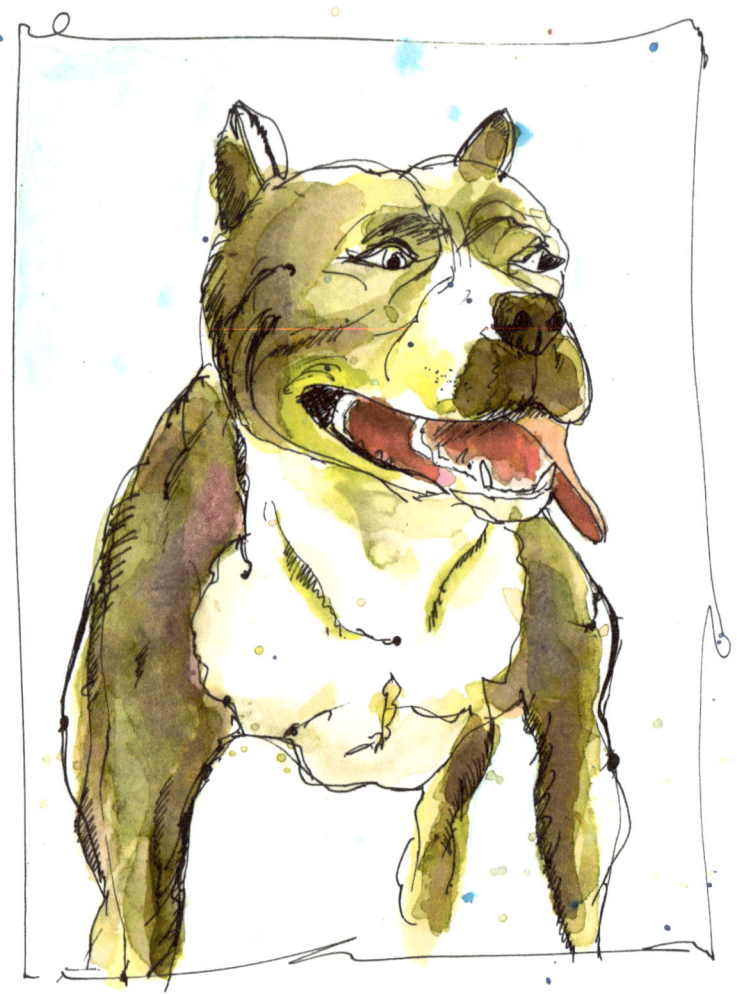

Toby

Los Angeles, California, USA

Toby here is the face of the national pitbull plight. Banned altogether in some US states, it is pitbulls like Toby that have the most trouble becoming adopted, often having to wait three times longer than other breeds. There is certainly a stigma attached to this breed, though many experts agree a loving and disciplined home can result in well behaved and well balanced dogs. So don't overlook a pitbull simply because of the label on the cage.

Jack

Lexington, Kentucky, USA

To say Jack's life began poorly is an understatement. After being tossed from a moving car as a one-year-old and breaking a leg, poor Jack ended up in a shelter in Lexington. It was here that things dramatically turned around. Buying dog food, and with no intention of adopting, Priscila had an immediate bond with the skinny and frightened Jack. A happy ending for Jack who now shares his wonderful life with rescue siblings Sara and Jojo.

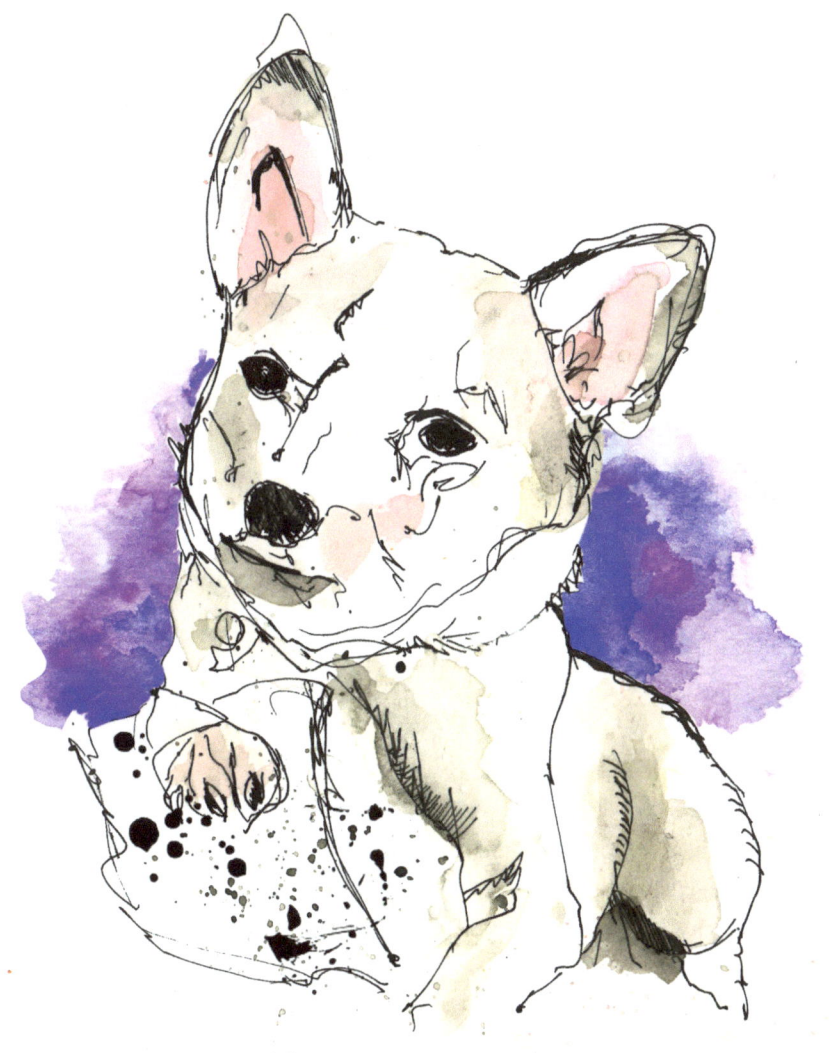

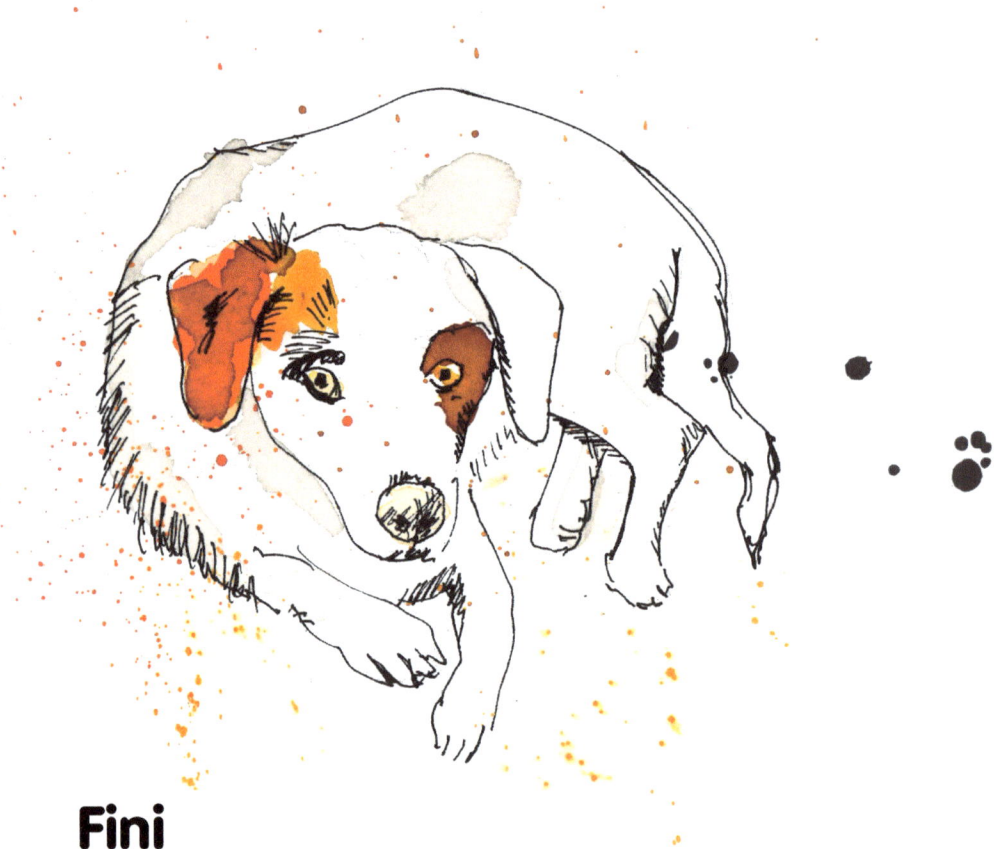

Fini

Mainz, Germany

Just like relationships in the human world, the first one doesn't always stick.
With good intentions, Mona went looking for a companion for her pup, Silverpaw.
In desperate need of a home, Fini looked like she was the answer, but unfortunately,
it just didn't work out. It happens! Fortunately Petra and her family graciously
stepped in and much to everyone's shock, were 'rewarded' for their kindness with a
litter of pups soon after!

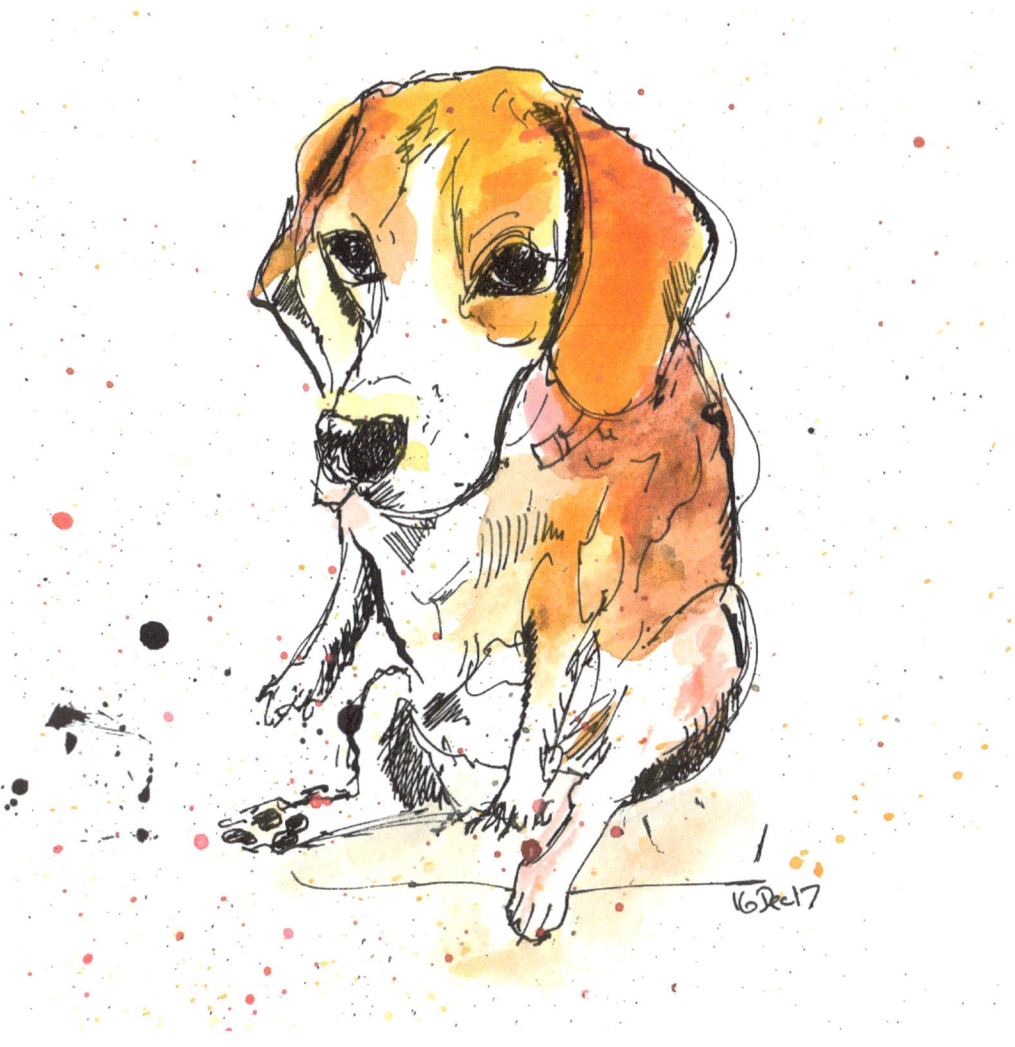

Maxine

Los Angeles, California, USA

Everyone loves a Beagle! Especially Mary Jane, who found poor Maxine, alone, terrified and shaking at the back of his cage in an LA pound. Maxine had been picked up, wandering the streets. But it was love at first site for Mary Jane and Maxine, and for the last 10 years little Max has been living the life of a queen – belly rubs, treats and long walks.

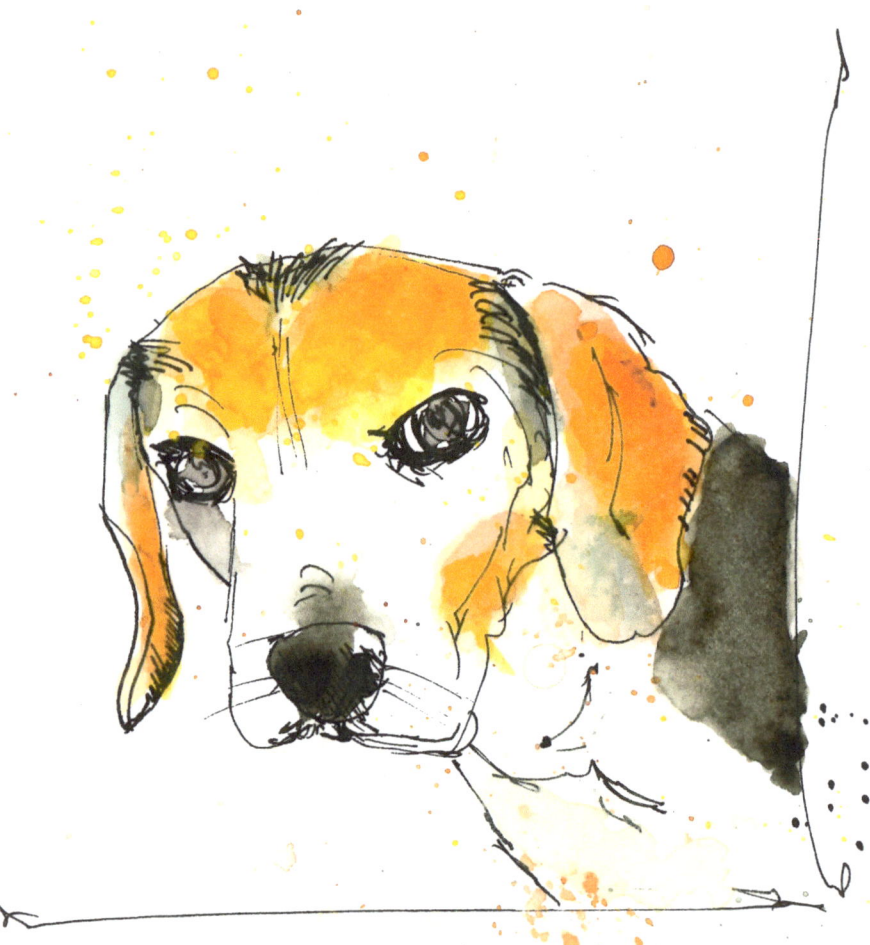

Sandy

New York, NY, USA

How do so many beautiful beagles end up in shelters?? "I'm moving and the new landlord won't have dogs". Well find somewhere else to move!! Poor Sandy ended up in a high kill shelter in New York due to her owner's apathy. A foster family came to her rescue, so is out of immediate danger. Danger that Sandy should never have faced.

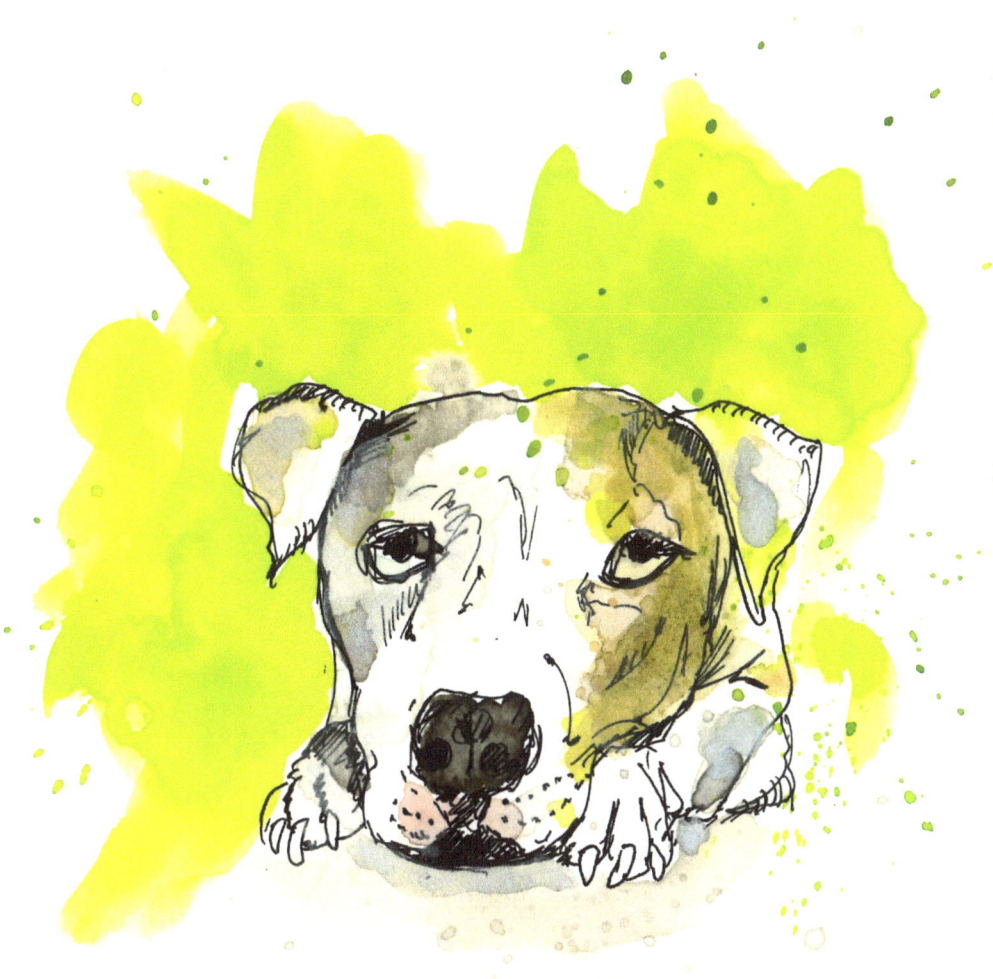

Buster Keaton

Chicago, Illinois, USA

Dogs don't belong on chains! Especially in front yards, in Chicago, in winter! Neighbour Elenor had had enough of seeing poor Buster freezing to death. Rather than doing anything illegal, Elenor simply approached the owner and offered to take Buster off his hands. Miraculously, he handed Buster over without argument. Buster now spends his winters snugly wrapped up indoors in front of an open fire.

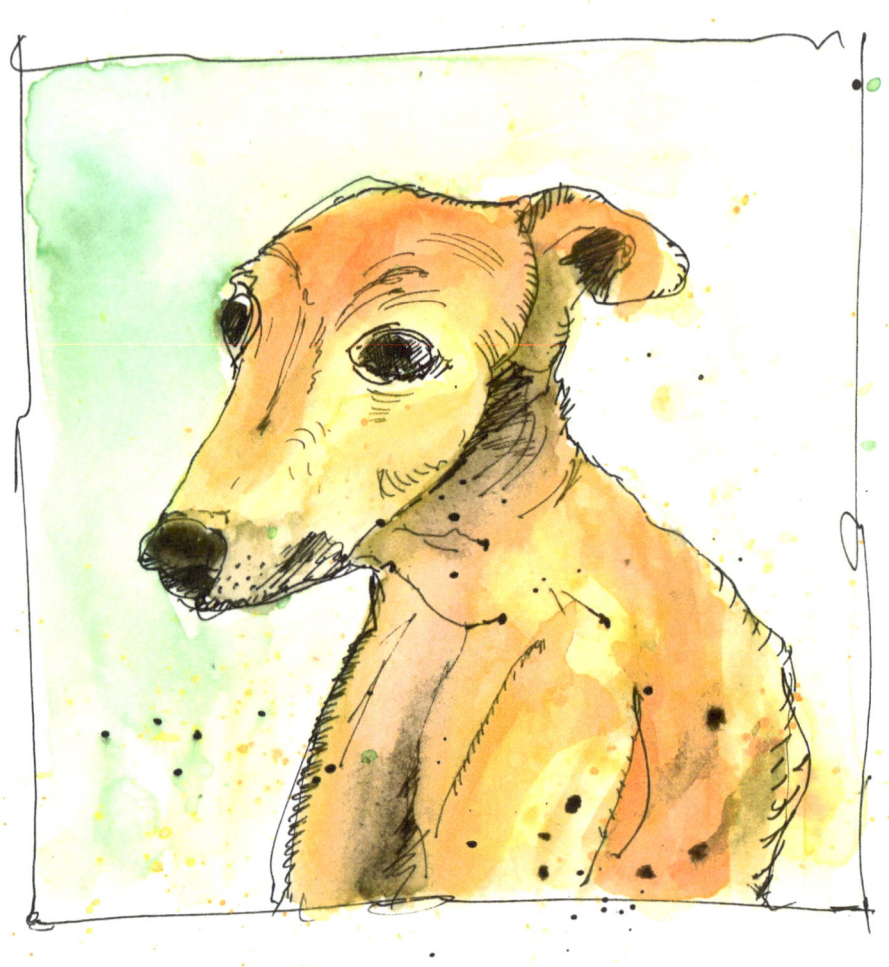

Humphrey

Sydney, Australia

Being fast doesn't necessarily guarantee a smooth passage through life. The plight of the modern greyhound – used then discarded. Fortunately there are outstanding organisations such as Greyhound Rescue in Sydney who facilitated Humphrey's transition from racer to family member. And parents Edina and Matthew are doing their bit for the greyhound fraternity – Humphrey has joined two new greyhound siblings!

Grohl

Ghana, West Africa.

Grohl (yes, named after Dave!) began life as a gift for his mom Malia, serving as a Peace Corps Volunteer in Ghana, West Africa at the time. As Malia moved from village to village working, young Grohl followed her around, chasing chickens and running from jungle predators. So concerned was Malia for Grohl's welfare, she put Grohl on the airplane with her when she returned stateside. Safe from the jungle, Grohl is now living it up on the beaches and mountains of Washington.

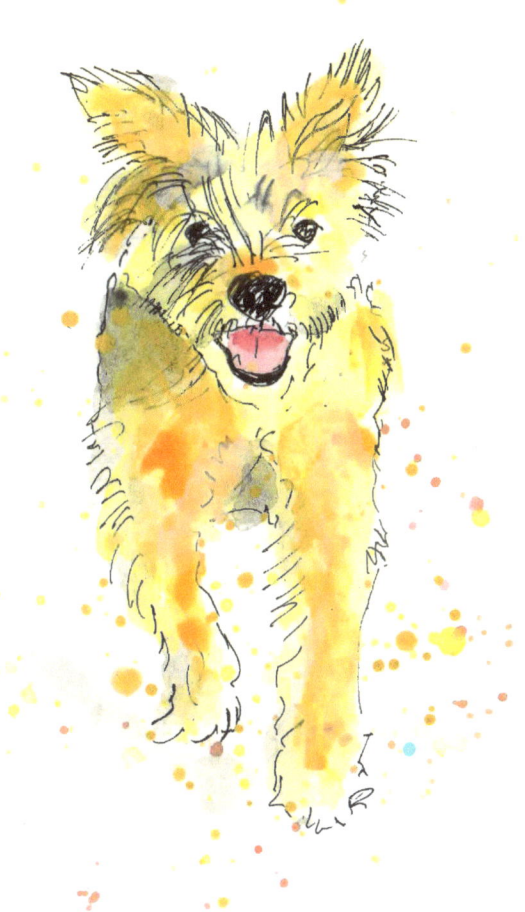

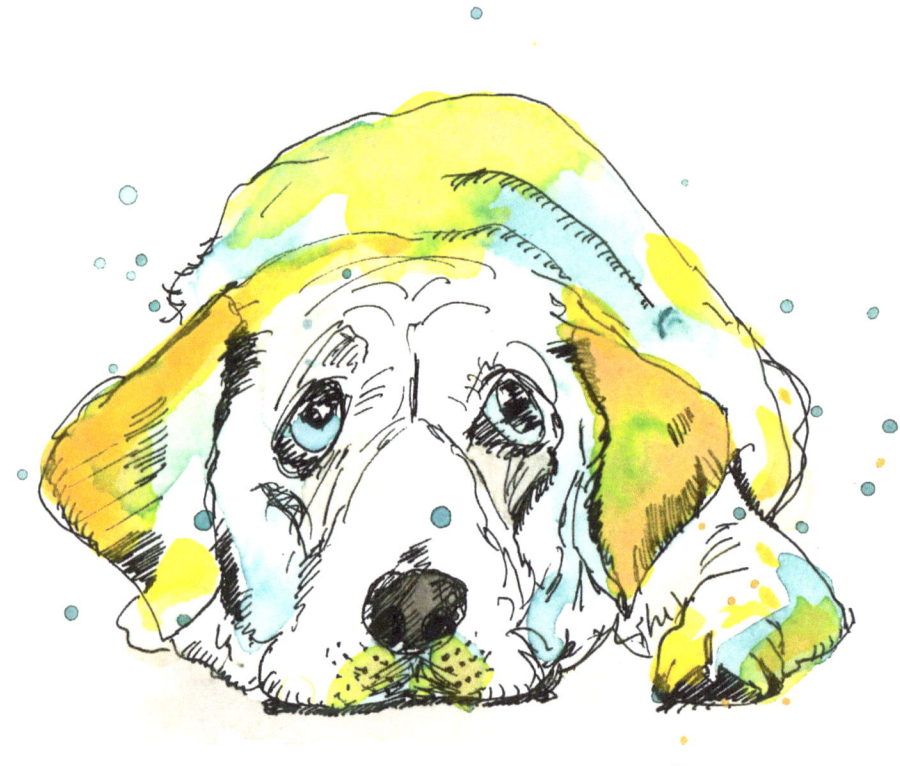

Elvis

Birmingham, England

Young Elvis here didn't quite get the same saloon passage through life as his illustrious namesake. Spending most of his life chained and outdoors, it took the courage of a desperate neighbour to call in authorities to save Elvis from his grisly existence. When they arrived they discovered the chain was wrapped around his neck so tightly that it had become embedded in his skin. The owner immediately gave up Elvis, and after emergency treatment, Elvis was placed in a permanent, loving home, where he hasn't seen a chain since.